To: Lorraine   With Love
From: Judy and Jane Eve
Christmas 2003

Provisions & Politics

Recipes Honoring First Lady Sarah Childress Polk
from the James K. Polk Memorial Association

Provisions and Politics
Recipes Honoring First Lady Sarah Childress Polk

Published by the James K. Polk Memorial Association

Copyright © 2003
James K. Polk Memorial Association
P.O. Box 741
Columbia, Tennessee 38402
931-388-2354

This cookbook is a collection of favorite recipes, which are not necessarily original recipes.

ISBN: 0-9728707-0-9
Library of Congress Control Number: 2003102897

Edited, Designed, and Manufactured by
Favorite Recipes® Press
an imprint of

FRP

P.O. Box 305142
Nashville, Tennessee 37230
800-358-0560

Art Director: Steve Newman
Book Design: Brad Whitfield and Susan Breining
Project Managers: Georgia Brazil and Tanis Westbrook
Project Editor: Debbie Van Mol

Manufactured in the United States of America
First Printing: 2003
5,000 copies

The James K. Polk Memorial Association Statement of Purpose
"The purpose of the organization shall be to operate, maintain, preserve and restore
The Polk Ancestral Home and its properties, its grounds and appurtenances,
and to perpetuate the memory of the eleventh President of the United States."

To

JOHN HOLTZAPPLE

Director, James K. Polk Ancestral Home

We dedicate this book as a tribute to his steadfast focus,
expertise and good humor in support of the Association's efforts to
"operate, maintain, preserve and restore"
that which has been entrusted to us.

September 4, 2003, marks the 200th anniversary of Sarah Childress Polk's birth.

To commemorate the occasion and honor the former First Lady,

*the James K. Polk Memorial Association has compiled **Provisions and Politics.***

The nonprofit Polk Association was founded in the 1920s to

"perpetuate the memory of the eleventh President of the United States"

and to preserve his surviving home in Columbia, Tennessee.

Although the organization's exhibits and programs focus on James K. Polk,

they necessarily tell the story of Sarah Polk, who played a crucial role

in her husband's political career.

Throughout her life, Sarah Polk surprised people.

Washington socialites were surprised that a lady from the Tennessee frontier

could be so sophisticated, stylish, and gracious. James K. Polk's male colleagues

were surprised that any woman could be so politically active and adept.

*Interspersed through **Provisions and Politics** are vignettes about Sarah Polk*

that might surprise modern readers who know nothing about this fascinating lady.

JOHN HOLTZAPPLE

Director, James K. Polk Ancestral Home

TABLE OF CONTENTS

DINING AT THE POLK WHITE HOUSE

Washington, Dec. 12, 1845.

We drove to the President's where we arrived at the moment . . . I had asked in vain and could hear of none of my acquaintance who were invited to the dinner and I found myself in a great company of all the Judges of the Supreme Court and their ladies and we were asked because we were on the Judiciary. Mrs. Polk received us in the circular blue room, furnished with gilded arm chairs and couches covered with blue and white satin damask. Mrs. Polk is very handsome in the evening, but a little too much the color of "refined gold" in the daytime, which Shakespeare insinuates needs no "gilding" but which in her case was decidedly improved by a scarlet cashmere turban embroidered in gold and trimmed with gold fringe on her "back hair" as Mr. Dickens calls it, and jetty ringlets in front. Her dress was dark blue velvet with Brussels lace trimming at the neck and under sleeves to match a long Brussels lace scarf reaching to the ground, nearly, around her neck. Scarlet bracelets confined sleeves at the wrist. Soon the august visitors began to fill the room and an aged lady next to my chair told me "the Judges always were late" and I began to feel goneness for want of dinner as I did not dare to eat one before leaving home.

I was very agreeably disappointed in the President. I had expected a tall, grim man and to my surprise found on entering the room a short, slender and pleasant looking gentleman with long silvery hair, bowing and congeeing about, shaking hands very cordially with Whigs and Democrats alike. To be sure he does not care now he's got it, but he might show a little spite to the Whigs if he wanted to do so. He resembles Mr. Jackson as a young hickory tree would a stiff old one. Mr. W. arranged the march to the dinner, the order of the polka. There were forty guests and the dinner table was as handsome as any I ever saw in proportion to its size, not even excepting the supper table at the Tuilleries at the Queen's Ball. The servants wore dark blue coats, white vests, cravats and gloves. There were two hundred chandeliers, candelabras and figures round the grand center ornament, all of which were of gilt burnished and very brilliant with vases of flowers.

The dining room is the west room of the right wing and corresponds to one-half of the east room. Three long windows were hung with purple and gold coloured figured curtains and purple velvet chairs with carved rosewood frames. As the furniture is all new and fresh and all the decorations newly gilded, it was very splendid. Sit! I guess we did sit, for four mortal hours, I judge 150 courses, for everything was in the French style and each dish a separate course.

Soup, fish, green peas, spinach, canvasback duck, turkey, birds, oyster pies, cotolettes di mouton, ham deliciously garnished, potatoes like snowballs, croquettes poulet in various forms, duck and olives, pate de foie gras, jellies, orange and lemon charlotte russe, ices, and "pink mud," oranges, grapes, prunes, sweetmeats, mottos and everything one can imagine, all served in silver dishes with silver tureens and wine coolers and the famous gold forks, knives and spoons for dessert. The China was white and gold and blue with a crest, the eagle of course, and the dessert plates were marine blue and gold with a painting in the center of fruits and flowers.

The President had to be so kind as to drink all our healths although we looked in pretty good case just then. The glassware was very handsome, blue and white finely cut, and pink champagne, gold sherry, green hock, madeira, the ruby port and sauterne formed a rainbow round each plate with the finger glasses and water decanters. Eating must end where repletion begins, and the finale with a number of mottos for each lady who boasted of her children, we danced the polka in reverse and reached the drawing room in safety. Coffee was served and liqueurs, and we said adieu and reached home at 10 o'clock.

— *From the diary of Mrs. J.E. Dixon, wife of James Dixon, Whig Representative from Connecticut, December 21, 1845. Typescript copy, James K. Polk Ancestral Home, Columbia, Tennessee.*

BRUNCHES AND LUNCHES

WEEKEND BRUNCH

Bellinis 34
Blueberry-Stuffed French Toast 142
Sausage and Bacon
Coffee

MOTHER'S DAY BRUNCH

Early's Cheese Wafers 16
Virginia's Crustless Crab Pie 108
or
Shrimp Cheesecake with Creole Mustard 114
Asparagus Tarragon 118
Slow-Roasted Tomatoes 128
Popovers 140
Macaroon Pudding 171

POLK SPRING PILGRIMAGE LUNCHEON

Welcome Wafers 16
Kile's Summer Punch 34
Tropical Chicken Salad 52
Asparagus Tarragon 118
Garlic Cheese Grits 131
Granny's Biscuits 138
Raspberry Cheesecake Brownies 176

FOURTH OF JULY COOKOUT

Avocado Salsa with Corn Chips 26
Beef Burgers Florentine 79
or
Grilled Marinated Lime Chicken 91
Fourth of July Marinated Vegetables 44
Steeplechase Potato Salad 50
Double Berry Shortcakes 161

PICNICS AND SUCH

ST. JOHN'S WHITSUNDAY PICNIC

Welcome Wafers   16
Sesame Shrimp   24
Cold Steak Salad with Caper Vinaigrette   51
Cajun Rice Salad   40
Victorian Fruit Salad   39
Light-as-a-Feather Italian Bread   146
Artichoke Mayonnaise   134
Plantation Cake   153
Claudia's Mint Tea   34

MULE DAY PICNIC

Roasted Garlic and Sun-Dried Tomato Cream Cheese with Crackers   32
Avocado Salsa with Corn Chips   26
Grilled Chili-Marinated Pork Tenderloin   83
Granny's Biscuits   138
New York Deli Slaw   46
Chicken and Artichoke Pasta Salad   53
Buttermilk Pie   162
Deep South Pralines   174
Carey's Brownies   177

TAILGATE PARTY

Tomato Soup with Pesto Swirl   69
Jordan's Cajun Beef Brisket with Boursin Cheese on Hard Rolls   74
Golden Wild Rice and Orzo Salad   40
Fruit and Cheese Tray
Best-Ever Chocolate Chip Cookies   178
Maury Molasses Cookies   181

SUPPERS

POLK PORCH SUPPER

We polled our Membership about their favorite recipes from the
James K. Polk Cookbook, published in 1978. These recipes received the most votes.
Filet of Beef   76
Garlic Cheese Grits   131
Squash Casserole   127
Fire and Ice Tomatoes   49
Polk Pickles   133
Pound Cake with Mixed Seasonal Berries and Zesty Lemon Sauce   156, 172

POOLSIDE SUMMER SUPPER

Sun-Dried Tomato and Pesto Boursin Torta   31
Volunteer Pork Tenderloin on Rolls   81
Crunchy Oriental Slaw   44
Green Rice   132
Marinated Vidalia Onions on Sliced Fresh Tomatoes   46
Yum Rum Cake   157
Maggie's Ice Cream Delights   165

WINTER SUPPER BY THE FIRE

Sausage Stars   20
Cold Weather Comfort Soup   67
Bay's Corn Bread   143
Iron Skillet Chocolate Pie   163

SPLURGE REPAIR SUPPER

Low-Fat Chicken Lasagna   92
Mixed Salad Greens with Vinaigrette Variations   59
Cantaloupe Sorbet   165

SUPER BOWL SUNDAY SUPPER

Pizzas on Party Rye 17
Kielbasa Normandy 21
Green Goddess Dip with Raw Vegetables 26
Mary Susan's Corn Dip 26
French Quarter Cheese Log with Crackers 30
Turkey Tortilla Soup 66
or
Delta Duck Gumbo 70
Bay's Corn Bread 143
Duck River Mud 177

COMFORT AND JOY, DELIVERED

Julia's Chicken Casserole 92
or
Monday's Chicken Chili 68
Alpine Braided Bread 145
Spinach and Strawberry Salad 47
Fruit Cobbler 164

GAME SUPPER

Duck Poppers 21
Bleu Cheese Mushrooms 19
Quail Stuffed with Oysters 98
or
Smothered Quail or Dove 99
Company Rice 133
Green Beans with Oven-Roasted Onion Slivers 122
Georgia's Biscuits 138
Dobosche Torte 152

11

CELEBRATIONS

NEW YEAR'S EVE DINNER PARTY

Caviar Crown Mold with Crackers 29
Northwest Saltimbocca of Beef with Bleu Cheese 75
or
Roasted Lamb Riblets 86
Roasted Rosemary Potatoes 125
Spinach Soufflé 126
Georgia's Biscuits 138
Strawberry-Glazed Cheesecake 160

VALENTINE'S DINNER FOR TWO

Eggs Colette 17
Halibut Sauté with Capers and Meunière Sauce 103
or
Billy's Simple Salmon 104
Artichoke Mayonnaise 134
Potatoes Anna 124
Asparagus Tarragon 118
Herb Crescent Rolls 138
Chocolate Almond Café au Lait 35

CINCO DE MAYO CELEBRATION

Gale's Corn and Black Bean Salsa with Corn Chips 27
Mexican Fiesta Chicken Platter 89
Corn Pudding 120
Fiesta Flan 170

DINNER WITH FRIENDS

Tzatziki with Pita Triangles and Raw Vegetables   26
Festive Fettuccini with Scallops and Red Pepper Cream Sauce   112
Eggless Caesar Salad   43
Light-as-a-Feather Italian Bread   146
Coffee-Toffee Meringue Delight   166

COCKTAIL PARTY BUFFET

Barbecued Pecans   33
Cold Braised Citrus Pork with Biscuits   22
Curried Won Ton Wonders   20
Crab Meat for a Crowd   25
Layered Brie with Bleu Cheese and Chutney,
Served with Apple Slices and Crackers   30
Mushroom Puffs   18
Chess Pie   162
Fudge Pie   162

This icon indicates favorite recipes chosen by the membership from
The James K. Polk Cookbook printed in 1978.

The Polk Home's detached kitchen was a bustle of activity in the 19th century. Separate from the main house to keep heat and damaging fire away from the living quarters, meals were cooked over an open hearth fireplace.

Savory Beginnings

WELCOME WAFERS

MAKES 2 DOZEN

3/4 cup (1 1/2 sticks) butter, softened
1/2 cup (2 ounces) shredded Cheddar cheese
1/3 cup bleu cheese
2 cups sifted flour
1 teaspoon chopped fresh parsley
1 teaspoon chopped fresh chives
1/2 garlic clove, minced

Beat the butter, Cheddar cheese and bleu cheese in a mixing bowl until creamy, scraping the bowl occasionally. Add the flour, parsley, chives and garlic and beat until mixed.

Shape the cheese mixture into 1 1/2-inch-thick logs. Chill, wrapped in plastic wrap, until firm. Cut each log into slices and arrange the slices cut side down on a baking sheet. Bake at 375 degrees for 8 to 10 minutes or until light brown. Remove to a wire rack to cool completely. Store in an airtight container. A preheated oven is recommended.

EARLY'S CHEESE WAFERS

MAKES 8 DOZEN

1 pound sharp Cheddar cheese, shredded
1/4 cup water
2 cups flour
3/4 cup finely chopped pecans
1/2 cup (1 stick) butter, softened
Tabasco sauce to taste
kosher salt to taste

Combine the cheese and water in a mixing bowl and beat until blended. Add the flour, pecans, butter and Tabasco sauce. Beat until mixed, scraping the bowl occasionally; the dough will be very stiff.

Divide the dough into 4 equal portions. Shape each portion into a log and wrap each log individually in waxed paper. Chill for 8 to 10 hours. Cut each log into 1/4-inch slices. Arrange the slices cut side down on a greased baking sheet. Bake at 325 degrees for 10 minutes or until light brown. Remove to a wire rack immediately and sprinkle lightly with kosher salt. Let stand until cool. Store in an airtight container. A preheated oven is recommended.

EGGS COLETTE
SERVES 8

RUSSIAN DRESSING

1 cup mayonnaise
1/4 cup chili sauce
1 tablespoon prepared horseradish
1 teaspoon Worcestershire sauce
1 teaspoon grated onion

EGGS

8 slices bread, lightly toasted and
crusts removed
24 to 32 Bibb lettuce leaves
8 hard-cooked eggs, sliced
1 small jar black or red caviar

For the dressing, combine the mayonnaise, chili sauce, horseradish, Worcestershire sauce and onion in a bowl and mix well.

For the eggs, arrange 1 bread slice on each of 8 salad plates. Layer each with 3 or 4 lettuce leaves and 1 sliced egg. Drizzle each with 2 to 3 tablespoons of the dressing and top with 1½ teaspoons of the caviar. Serve immediately.

PIZZAS ON PARTY RYE
MAKES 2 DOZEN

1 pound hot or mild sausage
1 pound ground beef
1/2 cup chopped onion
1 pound American cheese, shredded
1 tablespoon oregano, chopped
1 tablespoon Heinz 57 Steak Sauce
1½ teaspoons Worcestershire sauce
1/2 teaspoon garlic salt
2 loaves party rye bread

*B*rown the sausage and ground beef with the onion in a heavy skillet, stirring until the sausage and ground beef are crumbly; drain. Stir in the cheese, oregano, steak sauce, Worcestershire sauce and garlic salt. Cook until the cheese melts, stirring frequently.

Generously spread 1 side of each slice of bread with some of the sausage mixture. Arrange the slices on a baking sheet. Bake at 400 degrees for 3 to 5 minutes or until heated through. You may prepare in advance and store in the freezer. Bake just before serving. A preheated oven is recommended.

MUSHROOM PUFFS

MAKES 150 PUFFS

PUFFS

1 cup water   *1 cup flour*
1/2 cup (1 stick) butter,   *4 eggs*
cut into 8 pieces

MUSHROOM FILLING

6 tablespoons butter   *1 tablespoon flour*
3 tablespoons vegetable oil   *2 cups whipping cream*
1 1/2 pounds fresh mushrooms, minced   *1/2 teaspoon salt*
6 tablespoons minced shallots or   *1/4 teaspoon (heaping) pepper*
green onions   *9 tablespoons madeira*

For the puffs, bring the water and butter to a rolling boil in a medium saucepan. Add the flour all at once and mix well. Cook over low heat until the mixture forms a ball, stirring constantly. Remove from the heat. Add the eggs 1 at a time, mixing well after each addition. Drop the dough by heaping teaspoonfuls onto an ungreased baking sheet.

Bake at 400 degrees for 30 to 40 minutes or until golden brown. Let stand until cool. Split each puff into halves and scoop out the soft centers, discarding the centers.

For the filling, heat the butter and oil in a large skillet until the butter melts. Sauté the mushrooms and shallots in the butter mixture for 2 to 3 minutes. Stir in the flour. Cook for 2 to 3 minutes, stirring constantly. Remove from the heat. Add the whipping cream, salt and pepper gradually, stirring constantly. Return the skillet to the heat and bring the whipping cream mixture to a boil, stirring frequently. Boil until thickened and reduced in volume, stirring occasionally. Stir in the wine. Bring to a boil. Taste and adjust the seasonings. The filling should be fairly thick. Let stand until cool.

Arrange the puff shell halves cut side up on a baking sheet. Spoon some of the filling into each shell. Bake at 400 degrees until heated through. Prepare the filled shells in advance and store, covered, in the refrigerator. Filled shells may be frozen. Thaw in the refrigerator and reheat before serving. A preheated oven is recommended.

BLEU CHEESE MUSHROOMS
MAKES 2 DOZEN

1 pound small mushrooms (about 2 dozen)
2 tablespoons butter
3 ounces bleu cheese
3 ounces cream cheese, softened

Remove the stems from the mushrooms. Chop the stems. Cook the stems in the butter in a skillet over medium heat for 10 minutes, stirring frequently. Combine the stems, bleu cheese and cream cheese in a bowl and mix well. Spoon some of the cheese mixture into each mushroom cap.

Arrange the stuffed mushrooms on a rack in a broiler pan or in a large baking dish. Broil for 2 to 3 minutes or until brown. Serve immediately. A preheated oven is recommended.

After the Civil War, Sarah Polk wrote letters to her longtime acquaintance President Andrew Johnson on behalf of Southern friends and relatives who had applied to regain their U.S. citizenship. She also asked the President to provide government records to Henry S. Randall, an author who was planning to write a biography of James K. Polk. In a letter to Randall, Sarah described her relationship with Andrew Johnson: "During his term as Govr. of the State, Senator in Congress & Military Governor, I received from him marked attention. I believe that he will be disposed to extend to me any favor that will be consistent."

CURRIED WON TON WONDERS

MAKES 4 DOZEN

12 won ton wrappers, cut into quarters
vegetable oil
1/4 cup plus 2 tablespoons plain yogurt
1/4 cup savory chutney
3 tablespoons crunchy peanut butter
1 tablespoon fresh lime juice
1 teaspoon curry powder
1 pound boneless skinless chicken breasts,
cooked and finely chopped
1/4 cup chopped green onion tops

*B*rush 1 side of each won ton quarter with oil. Pat each won ton quarter oiled side up over the bottom and up the side of a miniature muffin cup. Bake at 325 degrees for 5 to 7 minutes or until light brown. Cool the won ton cups slightly before removing to a wire rack to cool completely. Cover tightly with plastic wrap or store in an airtight container for up to 3 days.

Combine the yogurt, chutney, peanut butter, lime juice and curry powder in a bowl and mix well. Stir in the chicken. Chill slightly. Spoon 1 heaping teaspoon of the chicken mixture into each won ton cup. Sprinkle with the green onion tops. Serve at room temperature, or heat if desired. A preheated oven is recommended.

SAUSAGE STARS

MAKES 200 STARS

1 pound sausage
4 cups (16 ounces) shredded Cheddar cheese
8 ounces cream cheese, softened
1 cup sour cream
1 (6-ounce) can pitted black olives,
drained and sliced
1 envelope ranch salad dressing mix
1 package won ton wrappers,
cut into quarters

*B*rown the sausage in a skillet, stirring until crumbly; drain. Stir in the Cheddar cheese, cream cheese, sour cream, olives and dressing mix. Press the won ton quarters over the bottoms and up the sides of miniature muffin cups sprayed with nonstick cooking spray. Spoon 1 tablespoon of the sausage mixture into each prepared muffin cup. Bake at 400 degrees for 10 minutes or until brown and bubbly. A preheated oven is recommended.

DUCK POPPERS

MAKES 16

2 wild duck breasts
1/2 cup Italian salad dressing or
favorite marinade
16 jalapeño chile slices
8 thick slices bacon, cut into halves

Cut the duck into 1/2- to 3/4-inch-thick strips, 3 to 4 inches long. Pour the dressing over the duck in a shallow dish, turning to coat. Marinate in the refrigerator for 30 to 60 minutes, turning occasionally. Place 1 jalapeño chile slice on each strip and roll to enclose. Wrap each roll with bacon and secure with a wooden pick.

Grill over medium-hot coals until the bacon is cooked through and the duck is medium, turning occasionally. For variety, add a strip of pepper Jack cheese with or without the jalapeño chile slice. You may substitute beef tenderloin, chicken or dove for the duck.

KIELBASA NORMANDY

SERVES 8

1 pound kielbasa, cut into 1-inch slices
1 cup dry white wine
2 tablespoons light brown sugar
2 tablespoons coarse grain mustard or
Dijon mustard
2 tablespoons Calvados
1/4 cup chopped fresh parsley

Cut each sausage slice into quarters. Arrange the sausage in a single layer in a large skillet. Pour the wine over the sausage. Bring to a boil. Cook for 12 minutes or until the wine almost evaporates, stirring occasionally. Stir in the brown sugar, mustard and liqueur. Cook for 1 minute, stirring constantly. Add the parsley and toss to mix. Serve warm or at room temperature with wooden picks and thinly sliced French bread for dipping.

COLD BRAISED CITRUS PORK
SERVES 12 TO 15

1 cup sherry
1 cup fresh orange juice
1/2 cup fresh lemon juice
1/2 cup olive oil
2 teaspoons grated lemon zest
2 teaspoons marjoram, crumbled
1 teaspoon cumin seeds
1 teaspoon ginger

2 bay leaves
2 boneless pork tenderloins
 (3 to 3 1/2 pounds total)
salt and freshly ground pepper to taste
2 tablespoons butter
1 to 2 tablespoons red currant jelly
1 to 2 teaspoons Dijon mustard
hot biscuits

*M*ix the sherry, orange juice, lemon juice, olive oil, lemon zest, marjoram, cumin seeds, ginger and bay leaves in a large shallow dish or sealable plastic bag. Add the pork tenderloins and turn to coat. Marinate, covered, in the refrigerator for 2 to 3 hours, turning frequently. Drain, reserving the marinade.

Pat the tenderloins with paper towels and sprinkle with salt and pepper. Heat the butter in a Dutch oven or heavy roasting pan over medium heat. Sear the tenderloins in the butter for 20 minutes or until brown on all sides. Add the reserved marinade to the Dutch oven. Bake, covered, at 325 degrees for 1 1/4 hours or until a meat thermometer inserted in the thickest portion of the tenderloin registers 165 to 170 degrees, basting frequently. Remove the tenderloins to a platter, reserving the pan liquids. Cool to room temperature. Chill, wrapped in foil, for up to 2 days.

Strain the pan liquids into a bowl, discarding the solids; chill. Skim the surface of the cooking liquid and pour into a saucepan. Bring to a simmer over medium heat. Stir in the jelly and Dijon mustard. Remove from the heat. Slice the chilled tenderloin and arrange on a serving platter. Pour the warm sauce over the pork. Serve with miniature biscuits. Refer to Georgia's Biscuits or Granny's Biscuits on page 138 for two good biscuit recipes. Cut the dough with miniature biscuit cutters when preparing for appetizers. A preheated oven is recommended.

SNACK-STYLE SHRIMP

S E R V E S   1 2

1/2 cup chopped celery tops
1/4 cup pickling spices
3 1/2 teaspoons salt
2 1/2 pounds frozen peeled large shrimp
2 cups sliced onions
7 or 8 bay leaves
1 1/4 cups olive oil
3/4 cup white vinegar
2 1/2 tablespoons undrained capers
2 1/2 teaspoons celery seeds
1 1/2 teaspoons salt
1/8 teaspoon hot pepper sauce

Bring enough water to a boil in a 5-quart stockpot to cover the shrimp generously. Add the celery tops, pickling spices and 3 1/2 teaspoons salt. Boil for 10 minutes. Add the frozen shrimp. Boil for 3 to 4 minutes or until the shrimp turn pink. Drain in a colander and rinse with cold water.

Alternate layers of the shrimp, sliced onions and bay leaves in a 2-quart dish until all the ingredients are used. Whisk the olive oil, vinegar, capers, celery seeds, 1 1/2 teaspoons salt and hot pepper sauce in a bowl until mixed. Pour the olive oil mixture over the prepared layers. Marinate, covered, in the refrigerator for 24 hours or longer. Discard the bay leaves. Serve using a slotted spoon. For variety, serve the marinated onions on party rye bread or rye crisps or in salads.

Someone who played an important role as guide and confidante for Sarah Polk was Dolley Madison. The fourth First Lady lived just across the lawn from the White House and was a regular companion to Mrs. Polk. In her seventies, Mrs. Madison was still the gauge of fashion in Washington society. Both First Ladies were fond of turbans. Together, Mrs. Madison and Mrs. Polk took long carriage rides into the country. They shared their experiences of being First Lady in an America at war, Madison during the War of 1812 when the White House was burned, Mrs. Polk during the Mexican-American War.

SESAME SHRIMP

MAKES 2 DOZEN

DIPPING SAUCE

1/2 cup mayonnaise
1/3 cup tahini
2 tablespoons sweet rice wine
2 tablespoons soy sauce

2 tablespoons seasoned rice vinegar
2 tablespoons lime juice
2 tablespoons grated fresh gingerroot
1 tablespoon sesame oil

SHRIMP

24 medium shrimp
2 teaspoons vegetable oil
1/4 teaspoon salt

1/8 teaspoon pepper
2 tablespoons white sesame seeds, or
1 teaspoon black sesame seeds

For the sauce, combine the mayonnaise, tahini, wine, soy sauce, vinegar, lime juice, gingerroot and sesame oil in a food processor. Process until smooth. Chill, covered, for 2 hours or for up to 3 days.

For the shrimp, peel and devein the shrimp, leaving the tails intact. Toss the shrimp with the oil, salt and pepper in a bowl. Dip 1 side of each shrimp in the sesame seeds. Arrange the shrimp sesame seed side up on a baking sheet lined with foil. Bake at 450 degrees for 5 to 7 minutes or until the shrimp are opaque. Serve warm with the sauce. You may store the sauce for up to 3 days in the refrigerator. The shrimp may be prepared up to 8 hours in advance and stored, covered, in the refrigerator. A preheated oven is recommended.

CRAB MEAT FOR A CROWD

SERVES 20

40 ounces cream cheese, softened
1 1/2 pounds lump white crab meat,
drained and shells and
cartilage removed
1 1/4 cups chopped onions
2 1/2 tablespoons grated horseradish
salt and black pepper to taste
cayenne pepper to taste
milk

Combine the cream cheese, crab meat, onions, horseradish, salt, black pepper and cayenne pepper in a bowl and mix well. Add milk until of dip consistency and mix well. Spoon the crab meat mixture into a baking dish. Bake at 350 degrees for 1 hour. Serve with corn chips and/or assorted party crackers. A preheated oven is recommended.

The first half of the 19th century saw great improvements in technology. While in the White House, the Polks oversaw the installation of gas lighting to replace the inadequate candlelight. Mrs. Polk, however, was not impressed with the gasoliers she had seen in the Capitol, thinking the light too harsh and dangerous. She insisted that the elegant chandeliers in the oval reception room remain. Her forethought proved beneficial, for during the first reception following its installation, the gas supply failed, and the White House was plunged into darkness, except for the reception room, where Sarah Polk stood illuminated under the "antiquated" candle-lit chandeliers.

TZATZIKI

S E R V E S   8   T O   1 0

1¹/2 large cucumbers, peeled and grated
2 cups sour cream
4 garlic cloves, finely chopped
¹/2 teaspoon salt
2 tablespoons extra-virgin olive oil
2 tablespoons white wine vinegar

Drain the cucumbers in a colander, pressing the cucumbers against the colander with a wooden spoon until most of the liquid drains out. Combine the sour cream, garlic and salt in a bowl and mix well. Stir in the cucumbers. Add the olive oil and vinegar and mix well. Chill, covered, for several hours to allow the flavors to blend. Serve with torn pita bread or assorted fresh vegetables.

MARY SUSAN'S CORN DIP

S E R V E S   4   T O   6

1 (11-ounce) can white Shoe Peg
corn, drained
³/4 cup (3 ounces) shredded Cheddar cheese
¹/2 cup (2 ounces) shredded Parmesan cheese
2 to 3 tablespoons mayonnaise
4 green onions, chopped

Combine all the ingredients in a bowl and mix well. Chill, covered, for 1 hour or longer to allow the flavors to blend. Serve with chips. You may adjust the amounts of all the ingredients except the corn to suit your taste.

GREEN GODDESS DIP

S E R V E S   8   T O   1 0

1³/4 cups mayonnaise
6 anchovy fillets
4 green onions with tops, cut into
1- to 2-inch pieces
2 shallots, cut into quarters
2 tablespoons tarragon vinegar
12 sprigs of parsley
2 sprigs of fresh tarragon, or 1 teaspoon
dried tarragon

Combine the mayonnaise, anchovies, green onions, shallots, vinegar, parsley and tarragon in a food processor. Process until smooth. Serve with assorted fresh vegetables.

AVOCADO SALSA

S E R V E S   8   T O   1 2

¹/2 avocado, chopped
juice of 1 lime
4 tomatoes, coarsely chopped
¹/2 red onion, chopped (optional)
¹/2 bunch cilantro, chopped
¹/2 teaspoon salt
1 jalapeño chile, seeded and
chopped (optional)

Drizzle the avocado with the lime juice in a bowl. Stir in the tomatoes, onion, cilantro, salt and jalapeño chile. Drain before serving. Serve with lime chips.

GALE'S CORN AND BLACK BEAN SALSA

S E R V E S 4 5

1 (28-ounce) can crushed tomatoes
2 (14-ounce) packages frozen whole
kernel corn
2 (15-ounce) cans black beans,
drained and rinsed
1 (14-ounce) can hearts of palm,
drained and sliced
1 medium onion, finely chopped
1 bunch cilantro, minced
1/3 cup vegetable oil
6 tablespoons fresh lime juice
1 tablespoon chili powder
1 teaspoon cumin

Combine the tomatoes, frozen corn, beans, hearts of palm, onion and cilantro in a bowl and mix well. Whisk the oil, lime juice, chili powder and cumin in a small bowl. Drizzle the oil mixture over the tomato mixture. Let stand, covered, for 1 hour or until the corn thaws, stirring occasionally. Serve as a dip with tortilla chips, or as a side dish. You may add chopped avocado if desired.

One of the frequent guests to the Polk White House was Missouri Senator Thomas Hart Benton. He was a rather boisterous politician who had once dueled with Andrew Jackson. At a formal White House dinner, as the guests waited beyond the proposed hour to be served, Benton quipped, "Mrs. Polk, did you not invite us to come and dine at a certain hour?" Without hesitation she replied, ". . . have you not lived in Washington long enough to know that the cooks fix the hour for dinner?" "Madame," Benton replied, "you have the advantage of me."

ORIENTAL EGGPLANT SALSA
SERVES 10 TO 12

2 (1- to 1¼-pound) eggplant
1 tablespoon vegetable oil or
 peanut oil
¾ cup (heaping) minced green onions
2½ tablespoons minced
 fresh gingerroot
4 garlic cloves, minced
1 teaspoon chili-garlic sauce
3 tablespoons light brown sugar
2 tablespoons soy sauce
1 tablespoon rice vinegar

juice of 1 lemon
2 large plum tomatoes, seeded and
 chopped
¾ cup packed finely chopped fresh
 cilantro
1½ teaspoons oriental sesame oil
salt and pepper to taste
1 tablespoon minced green onions
1 tablespoon finely chopped fresh
 cilantro

*P*ierce the surface of each eggplant with a fork and arrange the eggplant on a baking sheet. Roast at 425 degrees for 1 hour or until the eggplant are soft and deflated, turning once. Cool slightly. Cut the eggplant into halves and scoop the pulp into a colander. Drain for 30 minutes. Transfer the pulp to a food processor. Pulse until almost puréed.

Heat the oil in a large heavy skillet over medium-high heat. Stir in ¾ cup green onions, gingerroot, garlic and chili-garlic sauce. Sauté for 45 seconds or just until the green onions are tender. Stir in the brown sugar, soy sauce, vinegar and lemon juice. Bring to a simmer, stirring constantly. Stir in the eggplant purée.

Cook for 2 minutes or until heated through, stirring frequently. Remove from the heat. Stir in the tomatoes, ¾ cup cilantro and sesame oil. Season with salt and pepper. Spoon into a bowl. Sprinkle with 1 tablespoon green onions and 1 tablespoon cilantro. Serve at room temperature with assorted party crackers and/or pita crisps. You may prepare 1 day in advance and store, covered, in the refrigerator. Bring to room temperature before serving.

CAVIAR CROWN MOLD

SERVES 12 TO 15

1 envelope unflavored gelatin
1/4 cup cold water
4 hard-cooked eggs, chopped
1/2 cup mayonnaise
1/4 cup minced fresh parsley
1 green onion with top,
  finely chopped
1/4 teaspoon salt, or to taste
1/8 teaspoon pepper or Tabasco sauce
1 medium avocado, puréed

1 medium avocado, chopped
1 medium shallot, minced
2 tablespoons fresh lemon juice
2 tablespoons mayonnaise
1/8 teaspoon Tabasco sauce
salt to taste
1 cup sour cream
1/4 cup minced onion
1 (2-ounce) jar black caviar, drained
  and rinsed

*M*ix the gelatin and cold water in a small microwave-safe dish. Microwave on Low for 20 seconds and stir. One-third of the gelatin will be used in each of the 3 layers. Microwave as needed to soften between steps.

Combine the eggs, 1/2 cup mayonnaise, parsley, green onion, 1/4 teaspoon salt and pepper in a bowl and mix well. Stir in 1 1/2 tablespoons of the gelatin. Spread the egg mixture over the bottom of a 6-inch springform pan sprayed with nonstick cooking spray. Chill for 30 minutes.

Combine the avocados, shallot, lemon juice, 2 tablespoons mayonnaise, Tabasco sauce and salt to taste in a bowl and mix well. Stir in 1 1/2 tablespoons of the gelatin. Spread over the chilled layer. Chill for 30 minutes.

Drain the sour cream in a colander for 20 minutes. Mix the sour cream and onion in a bowl. Stir in the remaining 1 1/2 tablespoons gelatin. Spread the sour cream mixture over the prepared layers. Chill, covered, for 3 to 10 hours.

To serve, remove the side of the springform pan. Spread the caviar over the top of the mold. Serve with assorted party crackers, melba rounds and/or pumpernickel or party rye bread. Double the recipe for a larger crowd.

29

LAYERED BRIE WITH BLEU CHEESE AND CHUTNEY

S E R V E S   1 0

1 (4¹/2-inch) round Brie cheese
¹/3 pound bleu cheese, crumbled
¹/3 cup savory chutney or apricot preserves
2 tablespoons chopped pecans
2 tablespoons sliced almonds
sliced tart apples

Slice the Brie horizontally into halves. Spread the bleu cheese on the cut side of the bottom half. Top with the remaining half, cut side down. Remove the rind from the top with a sharp knife and discard.

Arrange the Brie on a microwave-safe plate. Spread the chutney over the top and sprinkle with the pecans and almonds. Chill, loosely covered, in the refrigerator. Microwave on Low for 2 to 3 minutes or until the Brie begins to soften just before serving. Serve with sliced apples and/or assorted party crackers.

FRENCH QUARTER CHEESE LOG

S E R V E S   6

8 ounces cream cheese, softened
1 tablespoon grated onion
1 garlic clove, minced
¹/2 teaspoon dill weed
1 cup chopped pecans, toasted
¹/4 cup (¹/2 stick) butter, melted
¹/4 cup packed dark brown sugar
1 teaspoon Worcestershire sauce
¹/2 teaspoon mustard

Mix the cream cheese, onion, garlic and dill weed in a bowl. Shape the cream cheese mixture into a log. Chill, wrapped in plastic wrap, until firm. Combine the pecans, butter, brown sugar, Worcestershire sauce and mustard in a saucepan and mix well. Heat until the brown sugar dissolves, stirring frequently. Remove from the heat and cool slightly. Arrange the cheese log on a serving platter and drizzle with the brown sugar sauce. Serve with assorted party crackers.

SUN-DRIED TOMATO AND PESTO BOURSIN TORTA

S E R V E S   1 2   T O   1 5

BASIL PESTO

3 medium garlic cloves
2 tablespoons pine nuts
1 cup fresh basil leaves (1¹/2 ounces)

¹/2 cup (2 ounces) freshly grated
Parmesan cheese
¹/3 cup extra-virgin olive oil

TORTA AND ASSEMBLY

1 (8-ounce) jar sun-dried tomatoes,
drained
24 ounces cream cheese, softened
6 tablespoons butter or margarine,
softened
4 large garlic cloves, crushed and
chopped
1 teaspoon thyme

1 teaspoon basil
1 teaspoon oregano
1 teaspoon dill weed
1 teaspoon marjoram
1 teaspoon salt-free seasoning mix
¹/3 teaspoon freshly ground pepper
1 sprig of basil

For the pesto, add the garlic cloves 1 at a time to a food processor, processing constantly until finely chopped. Add the pine nuts, basil and cheese. Process until the basil is chopped. Add the olive oil gradually, processing constantly until blended and scraping the side of the bowl as needed. Spoon the pesto into a covered container. Store in the refrigerator for up to 2 days. Bring to room temperature before using.

For the torta, line a loaf pan with plastic wrap, allowing enough overhang to cover the torta. Pat the sun-dried tomatoes with paper towels and chop. Beat the cream cheese and butter in a mixing bowl until smooth, scraping the bowl occasionally. Add the garlic, thyme, basil, oregano, dill weed, marjoram, salt-free seasoning mix and pepper to the cream cheese mixture and beat until blended. Chill, covered, for 15 minutes.

Spread half the cream cheese mixture in the prepared loaf pan. Spread with the pesto. Sprinkle with ¹/4 cup of the sun-dried tomatoes. Layer with the remaining cream cheese mixture and smooth with a knife. Cover with the plastic wrap. Chill for 4 hours or longer.

Invert the torta onto a serving platter, discarding the plastic wrap. Sprinkle with the remaining sun-dried tomatoes and top with the sprig of basil. Serve with assorted party crackers. You may substitute one 3- or 4-ounce jar of commercially prepared basil pesto for the homemade pesto.

SUN-DRIED TOMATO PESTO

MAKES 1 CUP

3 to 4 tablespoons pine nuts
1 (8-ounce) jar oil-pack sun-dried tomatoes
1/4 cup fresh basil leaves
4 or 5 garlic cloves
2 tablespoons extra-virgin olive oil
salt and pepper to taste

Spread the pine nuts in a single layer on a baking sheet. Toast at 350 degrees for 5 minutes, stirring frequently. Remove to a plate to cool. Process the pine nuts, undrained sun-dried tomatoes, basil, garlic, olive oil, salt and pepper in a food processor until smooth. Serve with thin crusty baguette slices or assorted fresh vegetables. A preheated oven is recommended.

ROASTED GARLIC AND SUN-DRIED TOMATO CREAM CHEESE

SERVES 8 TO 10

1 small to medium head garlic
olive oil
8 ounces tub-style light cream cheese
1/4 cup chopped drained oil-pack
sun-dried tomatoes
1 tablespoon chopped green onion
1/4 teaspoon cayenne pepper

Slice the top off the head of the garlic and discard. Arrange the garlic on a baking sheet. Drizzle with olive oil and roast at 250 to 300 degrees for 30 to 40 minutes or until the garlic is soft. Squeeze the garlic into a bowl and mash.

Invert the cream cheese onto a platter. Top with the roasted garlic and sun-dried tomatoes and sprinkle with the chopped green onion and cayenne pepper. Serve with assorted party crackers. A preheated oven is recommended.

BARBECUED PECANS
MAKES 4 CUPS

2 tablespoons butter
1/4 cup Worcestershire sauce
1 tablespoon ketchup
1/4 teaspoon hot sauce
4 cups pecan halves
salt to taste

Heat the butter in a heavy saucepan until melted. Remove from the heat. Stir in the Worcestershire sauce, ketchup and hot sauce. Add the pecans and stir until coated.

Spread the pecans in a single layer on a baking sheet. Bake at 400 degrees for 13 to 15 minutes, stirring every 5 minutes. Remove the pecans to paper towels to drain and sprinkle with salt. Let stand until cool. Delicious sprinkled on ice cream with chocolate or caramel sauce. Makes terrific Christmas gifts. A preheated oven is recommended.

SWEET SPICED PECANS
MAKES 3 CUPS

1 egg white
3 cups pecan halves
1/3 cup sugar
2 teaspoons cinnamon
1/2 teaspoon allspice
1/2 teaspoon seasoned salt
1/4 teaspoon nutmeg

Beat the egg white in a mixing bowl until foamy. Add the pecans to the egg white and toss to coat. Mix the sugar, cinnamon, allspice, seasoned salt and nutmeg in a bowl. Add the pecans and toss to coat.

Spread the pecans in a single layer on a lightly greased baking sheet. Bake at 250 degrees for 1 hour. Cool slightly and break into bite-size pieces. Let stand until cool. Store in an airtight container. A preheated oven is recommended.

BELLINIS

S E R V E S   2

2 ounces peach nectar
1 ounce peach schnapps
1 teaspoon fresh lemon juice
1/2 cup ice
3 ounces Champagne

*P*rocess the nectar, schnapps and lemon juice in a blender until frothy. Add the ice. Pulse for several seconds. Add half the nectar mixture and half the Champagne to each of 2 flutes and stir.

TROPICAL RUM CHUM

S E R V E S   6

1 (46-ounce) can pineapple juice
1 (6-ounce) can frozen limeade concentrate
6 ounces (more or less) rum
6 maraschino cherries

Combine the pineapple juice, limeade concentrate and rum in a freezer container and mix well. Freeze, covered, until slushy. Let stand at room temperature until of a slushy consistency. Place 1 cherry in each of 6 glasses. Divide the slush mixture evenly between the glasses.

KILE'S SUMMER PUNCH

S E R V E S   1 5

2 quarts cranberry juice with peach
1 quart orange juice
1 (20-ounce) bottle lemon-lime soda
juice of 2 limes
lime slices
maraschino cherries

*M*ix the cranberry juice, orange juice, soda and lime juice in a 1-gallon container. Pour over crushed ice in glasses. Garnish each serving with a lime slice and maraschino cherry. You may substitute two 8-ounce bottles Perrier for the soda for a less sweet punch.

CLAUDIA'S MINT TEA

M A K E S   1   G A L L O N

10 tea bags, or 4 family-size tea bags
2/3 cup (scant) sugar
1 cup lemonade mix (not sugar free)
10 sprigs (or more) of fresh mint
1 quart boiling water

*C*ombine the tea bags, sugar, lemonade mix and mint in a heatproof pitcher. Add the boiling water. Steep for 30 minutes. Strain the tea into a 1-gallon container. Add enough cold water to fill the container. Pour over ice in glasses. For variety, add one 6-ounce can pineapple juice.

CHOCOLATE ALMOND CAFÉ AU LAIT

SERVES 4 TO 6

2 cups chocolate milk
2 tablespoons almond liqueur, or
1 teaspoon almond extract
2 teaspoons sugar
2 cups hot strong coffee (3/4 cup coffee granules to
3 cups water)
1/2 cup heavy whipping cream
1 tablespoon confectioners' sugar
1/2 teaspoon vanilla extract
chocolate curls

Heat the chocolate milk in a saucepan over medium-low heat for 5 minutes or until bubbles form around the edge of the pan; do not boil. Stir in the liqueur and sugar. Remove from the heat. Pour the coffee into a heatproof pitcher or carafe. Add the chocolate milk mixture and stir.

Beat the whipping cream, confectioners' sugar and vanilla in a mixing bowl until stiff peaks form. Pour the café into a mug. Top each serving with whipped cream and chocolate curls.

Henry Clay, whom Polk defeated for the Presidency, once came to dine at the White House. Seated next to Mrs. Polk, he stated, "Madame, I must say that in my travels . . . I have heard but one opinion of you. All agree in commending in the highest terms your excellent administration of the domestic affairs of the White House. "But," he continued, directing his attention to President Polk, "as for that young gentleman there, I cannot say as much." "Indeed," said Mrs. Polk, "I am glad to hear that my administration is popular. And in return for your compliment, I will say that if the country should elect a Whig next fall, I know of no one whose elevation would please me more than that of Henry Clay."

The parlor was the entertainment center of the home. Elegant furnishings were purchased by the Polks in New York City. Besides the beautiful French vases and chandelier, the Polks filled their parlor with mementos of their political lives, including prints and White House portraits painted by G.P.A. Healy.

Bountiful Salads

GRIFF'S CRANBERRY SALAD
S E R V E S 4 T O 6

2 cups fresh cranberries
1 envelope unflavored gelatin
2/3 cup cold water
1 (8-ounce) can juice-pack crushed pineapple
3/4 cup sugar
2 oranges, peeled, seeded and chopped
1 cup chopped pecans

*R*inse the cranberries. Process the cranberries in a food processor or blender until ground. Soften the gelatin in the cold water. Drain the pineapple, reserving the juice.

Heat the reserved pineapple juice and gelatin mixture in a saucepan until the gelatin dissolves, stirring frequently. Remove from the heat. Combine the pineapple, cranberries, sugar and oranges in a bowl and mix well. Stir in the pineapple juice mixture and pecans. Spoon the gelatin mixture into a greased mold. Chill until set.

GRAPEFRUIT SALAD
S E R V E S 8 T O 1 0

TOPPING

1/2 cup mayonnaise
1/4 cup sour cream
1 teaspoon sugar
1/4 teaspoon mace
grated orange zest

SALAD

1 (3-ounce) package lemon gelatin
1 cup hot ginger ale
1 tablespoon vinegar
1 tablespoon sugar
1/2 teaspoon salt
sections of 1 large grapefruit
1 (8-ounce) can crushed pineapple, drained
1/2 cup slivered almonds, toasted

For the topping, combine the mayonnaise, sour cream, sugar, mace and orange zest in a bowl and mix well. Chill, covered, in the refrigerator.

For the salad, dissolve the gelatin in the hot ginger ale in a heatproof bowl. Stir in the vinegar, sugar and salt. Let stand until cool. Cut each grapefruit section into 3 pieces. Add the grapefruit, pineapple and almonds to the gelatin mixture and mix well. Pour into lightly greased individual molds. Chill until set. Invert the molds onto individual salad plates and top each with a dollop of the topping.

FESTIVE POMEGRANATE AND PEAR SALAD

S E R V E S   6

1 pomegranate
3 green pears, peeled and cut into
bite-size pieces
2 tablespoons lime juice
2 tablespoons minced fresh tarragon
lettuce leaves

Cut the pomegranate into several sections with a sharp knife. Pry out the seeds, discarding any of the membrane that may adhere to the seeds. Combine the pomegranate seeds, pears, lime juice and tarragon in a bowl and mix well. Chill, covered, for 30 minutes or longer. Spoon onto lettuce-lined salad plates.

VICTORIAN FRUIT SALAD

S E R V E S   1 6

3/4 cup sugar
3 eggs, beaten
3 tablespoons butter, softened
1/2 cup lemon juice
3 Golden Delicious apples,
peeled and chopped
3 Red Delicious apples, peeled and chopped
1 tablespoon lemon juice
1 (20-ounce) can juice-pack pineapple tidbits,
drained
1 bunch seedless green grapes, separated
1 bunch seedless red grapes, separated
1 1/2 cups miniature marshmallows
1/2 cup chopped walnuts

Combine the sugar, eggs and butter in a saucepan. Stir in 1/2 cup lemon juice. Cook over medium heat until thickened, stirring constantly. Chill until cool.

Toss the apples with 1 tablespoon lemon juice in a serving bowl. Add the pineapple, grapes, marshmallows, walnuts and chilled dressing to the apple mixture and toss to mix. Chill, covered, until serving time.

GOLDEN WILD RICE AND ORZO SALAD

S E R V E S   6   T O   8

VINAIGRETTE
1/4 cup olive oil
1/4 cup white wine vinegar
1 tablespoon sugar
1/4 teaspoon red pepper flakes
1/4 teaspoon oregano
salt and ground black pepper to taste

SALAD
2/3 cup wild rice
2/3 cup orzo
1 (11-ounce) can Shoe Peg corn, drained
3/4 cup minced yellow bell pepper
1/4 cup currants
chopped fresh parsley

For the vinaigrette, combine the olive oil, vinegar, sugar, red pepper flakes, oregano, salt and black pepper in a jar with a tight-fitting lid and seal tightly. Shake to mix.

For the salad, cook the wild rice using package directions; drain. Cook the pasta using package directions until al dente; drain. Combine the wild rice, pasta, corn, bell pepper, currants and a generous amount of parsley in a bowl and mix well. Add the desired amount of the vinaigrette and toss to coat. Chill, covered, for 2 to 3 hours before serving.

CAJUN RICE SALAD

S E R V E S   8   T O   1 0

CAJUN DRESSING
3 tablespoons olive oil
2 tablespoons white wine vinegar or white vinegar
2 tablespoons prepared Creole mustard or Dijon mustard
4 hard-cooked eggs, chopped
1 cup crumbled crisp-cooked bacon (optional)
1/2 cup chopped dill pickles
salt and freshly ground black pepper to taste
cayenne pepper to taste

SALAD
3 cups cooked rice (cooked in chicken broth)
2/3 cup black olives or pimento-stuffed green olives, chopped
1/2 cup chopped celery
1/2 cup chopped onion
1/2 cup chopped shallots

For the dressing, whisk the olive oil, vinegar and Creole mustard in a large bowl. Stir in the eggs, bacon and pickles. Season with salt, black pepper and cayenne pepper.

For the salad, add the rice, olives, celery, onion and shallots to the dressing and toss gently to coat. Chill, covered, in the refrigerator for 2 hours or longer.

ARTICHOKE CHARLESTON

S E R V E S   1

DIJON VINAIGRETTE

1 tablespoon white wine vinegar
1 tablespoon red wine vinegar
1 tablespoon chives
1 teaspoon sugar
1 teaspoon Dijon mustard
1 garlic clove, crushed
1/2 teaspoon salt
1/4 teaspoon freshly ground pepper
1/4 teaspoon balsamic vinegar
1/2 cup olive oil

SALAD

1 artichoke
lemon slices
1/2 tomato, chopped
spring mix salad greens
1 red onion, slivered

For the vinaigrette, mix all the ingredients except the olive oil in a microwave-safe bowl. Add the olive oil gradually, whisking constantly. Microwave for 30 seconds and stir. Cover to keep warm.

For the salad, place the artichoke upright in a microwave-safe bowl. Add the lemon slices and enough water to measure 1 inch. Microwave, covered with plastic wrap, on High for 8 minutes or until the leaves can be easily removed. Let stand until cool. Spread the leaves of the artichoke out like a flower. Remove the inner leaves intact and reserve. Cut out the choke. Pile the chopped tomato in the center of the artichoke and place the reserved leaves on top. Toss the spring mix with the onion on a serving plate. Add the artichoke and drizzle with the warm vinaigrette. Serve with sliced French bread.

During a reception at the White House with the parlor filled with people, there fell a sudden silence when a gentleman said to Sarah Polk, "Madame, I have long wished to see the lady upon whom the Bible pronounces a woe!" The remark startled onlookers as Mrs. Polk returned a puzzled look at the gentleman. He then continued, "Does not the Bible say, 'Woe unto you when all men shall speak well of you?'" A collective sigh of relief filled the room as Mrs. Polk bowed in thanks for the compliment.

CHICK-PEA SALAD

S E R V E S   8

4 cups canned chick-peas,
rinsed and drained
1 cup coarsely chopped celery
1/2 cup chopped drained sauerkraut
1/4 cup finely chopped pimento
1 cup chopped onion
1/2 cup vinegar
1/2 cup sugar
1/2 cup vegetable oil

Combine the chick-peas, celery, sauerkraut and pimento in a bowl and mix gently. Bring the onion, vinegar and sugar to a boil in a saucepan, stirring occasionally. Remove from the heat. Stir in the oil. Pour the vinegar mixture over the chick-pea mixture and toss to coat. Spoon into a glass container. Chill, covered, for 8 to 10 hours. Drain before serving. Serve with pork, game or other dark meat.

BOK CHOY SALAD

S E R V E S   6   T O   8

1 (3-ounce) package ramen noodles
1/2 cup sunflower kernels
3 tablespoons slivered almonds
1/2 cup sugar
1/4 cup olive oil
1/4 cup cider vinegar
2 tablespoons soy sauce
1 bok choy, shredded
6 green onions, chopped

Discard the flavor packet from the noodles. Crumble the noodles into a bowl. Stir in the sunflower kernels and almonds. Spread the almond mixture on a baking sheet. Toast at 350 degrees for 8 to 10 minutes or until light brown. Remove to a platter to cool.

Bring the sugar, olive oil, vinegar and soy sauce to a boil in a saucepan over medium heat, stirring occasionally. Remove from the heat. Let stand until cool. Toss the bok choy and green onions in a large bowl. Add the almond mixture and olive oil mixture and toss to mix. Serve immediately. A preheated oven is recommended.

EGGLESS CAESAR SALAD

S E R V E S   6

CAESAR DRESSING

1 (1/2- to 1-ounce) can anchovies, or
2 tablespoons anchovy paste (optional)
3 tablespoons Dijon mustard
1 tablespoon oregano
2 teaspoons minced garlic
2 teaspoons freshly cracked pepper
1/4 teaspoon salt
1/4 cup red wine vinegar
1 cup olive oil

SALAD

1/2 head romaine, torn into bite-size pieces
1/2 head red leaf lettuce, torn into
bite-size pieces
1/2 cup seedless red grape halves
2 tablespoons grated Parmesan cheese
3/4 cup croutons

For the dressing, process the anchovies in a food processor until puréed. Add the Dijon mustard, oregano, garlic, pepper and salt. Process until mixed. Add the vinegar gradually, processing constantly until blended. Add the olive oil gradually, processing constantly until the dressing is thick and creamy. Store, covered, in the refrigerator.

For the salad, toss the romaine, red leaf lettuce, grapes, cheese and croutons in a bowl. Add the dressing and toss to coat. Serve immediately.

LAYERED GREEK SALAD

S E R V E S   6

4 slices dry garlic toast (sourdough
bread preferred), cubed
1/2 to 1 head lettuce, chopped (6 cups)
4 romaine leaves, chopped
3 large tomatoes, chopped
3/4 cup chopped red bell pepper
1/2 cup julienned purple onion
1/3 cup sliced black olives
1 rib celery, chopped
1/2 cup crumbled feta cheese
1/2 cup Italian dressing
coarsely ground pepper to taste

*S*pread the garlic toast cubes over the bottom of a 2- or 3-quart salad bowl. Layer with the chopped lettuce and romaine. Toss the tomatoes, bell pepper, onion, olives and celery gently in a bowl. Spoon the tomato mixture over the prepared layers and sprinkle with the cheese. Drizzle with the dressing and sprinkle with pepper. Toss just before serving. You may prepare several hours in advance and store, covered, in the refrigerator. Add the dressing just before serving.

FOURTH OF JULY MARINATED VEGETABLES

S E R V E S 1 2

2 (16-ounce) cans white corn, drained
2 (16-ounce) cans French-cut green
beans, drained
1 cup thinly sliced red or white onion
1 cup chopped red or green bell pepper or
combination of the two
3/4 cup sliced celery
1 cup sugar
1/2 cup vegetable oil
1/2 cup apple cider vinegar
1 teaspoon salt
1/2 teaspoon pepper

Combine the corn, beans, onion, bell pepper and celery in a bowl and mix gently. Whisk the sugar, oil, vinegar, salt and pepper in a bowl until mixed. Add the oil mixture to the corn mixture and stir gently. Marinate, covered, in the refrigerator for 8 to 10 hours, stirring once or twice.

CRUNCHY ORIENTAL SLAW

S E R V E S 1 2

2 packages chicken-flavored ramen noodles
2 (16-ounce) packages shredded
cabbage slaw
1 cup sunflower kernels
1 cup slivered almonds, toasted
5 green onions, chopped
1/2 cup sugar
1/2 cup vegetable oil
1/3 cup cider vinegar

Reserve the flavor packets from the noodles. Crush the noodles. Toss the noodles, slaw, sunflower kernels, almonds and green onions in a salad bowl. Whisk the contents of the reserved flavor packets, sugar, oil and vinegar in a bowl until mixed. Add the oil mixture to the slaw mixture and toss to coat. Serve immediately. You may prepare the salad in advance, adding the noodles just before serving.

SARAH'S SALAD TOSS
VARIABLE

SPICY PECANS
2 tablespoons sugar
1/2 cup warm water
1 cup pecan halves or pieces
2 tablespoons sugar
1 tablespoon chili powder
1/8 teaspoon red pepper flakes

BALSAMIC VINAIGRETTE
1/2 cup olive oil
1/4 cup balsamic vinegar
1 1/2 tablespoons Dijon mustard
1 1/2 tablespoons honey
1 garlic clove, minced
1/8 teaspoon pepper

SALAD
mixed salad greens
crumbled bleu cheese
1 (11- or 16-ounce) can mandarin oranges, drained
fresh strawberries

For the pecans, dissolve 2 tablespoons sugar in the warm water in a bowl. Stir in the pecans. Let stand for 10 minutes; drain. Mix 2 tablespoons sugar, chili powder and red pepper flakes in a shallow dish. Add the pecans and toss to coat. Bake the pecans in a single layer on a lightly greased baking sheet at 350 degrees for 10 minutes, stirring occasionally.

For the vinaigrette, combine all the ingredients in a jar with a tight-fitting lid; seal tightly and shake to mix.

For the salad, toss the salad greens, bleu cheese, mandarin oranges and strawberries in a salad bowl. Drizzle lightly with the vinaigrette and top with the pecans. Serve immediately.

President and Mrs. Polk rarely left Washington during their four years there. On one occasion, however, while the President took a two-week political tour into the Northeast, Sarah took the opportunity to return to Tennessee. She spent time with family in Murfreesboro, but also used the time to inspect the construction work on Polk Place, their retirement home in Nashville. Sarah carefully recorded the dimensions of floors, walls, and windows, then upon her return east, began ordering material, wallpapers, and carpeting through Alexander Stewart's famed department store in New York City.

NEW YORK DELI SLAW

S E R V E S   8   T O   1 0

SLAW
1 medium head cabbage
1 green bell pepper, chopped
2 bunches spring onions, chopped

CREAMY SLAW DRESSING
3 tablespoons apple cider vinegar
1 tablespoon water
2 teaspoons sugar
1 1/2 cups mayonnaise
1 tablespoon (or more)
horseradish (optional)
salt to taste

For the slaw, chop the cabbage finely by hand. Toss the cabbage, bell pepper and spring onions in a large salad bowl.

For the dressing, combine the vinegar, water and sugar in a small saucepan. Bring to a boil, stirring occasionally. Boil just until the sugar dissolves, stirring frequently. Combine just enough of the vinegar mixture with the mayonnaise in a bowl until the mixture is creamy, not watery. The mayonnaise mixture should have a sweet-sour taste. Add additional vinegar mixture if too sweet. Stir in the horseradish. Add the dressing to the slaw and toss to coat. Season with salt.

MARINATED VIDALIA ONIONS

V A R I A B L E

4 large Vidalia onions, thinly sliced and
separated into rings
2 cups water
1 cup sugar
1/2 cup white vinegar
1/2 cup mayonnaise
juice of 1/2 lemon
parsley flakes to taste
celery salt to taste
paprika to taste
Beau Monde seasoning to taste
sliced tomatoes

*P*lace the onions in a bowl. Bring the water, sugar and vinegar to a boil in a saucepan. Boil until the sugar dissolves, stirring frequently. Pour the vinegar mixture over the onions. Let stand until cool. Marinate, covered, in the refrigerator for 8 to 10 hours, stirring occasionally; drain well.

Combine the mayonnaise, lemon juice, parsley flakes, celery salt, paprika and Beau Monde seasoning in a bowl and mix well. Add the mayonnaise mixture to the onions and mix well. Store, covered, in the refrigerator for several days. Serve as desired over sliced fresh tomatoes.

BACON, EGG AND SPINACH SALAD

S E R V E S   8

CREAMY RED WINE DRESSING

1 cup canola oil (do not use olive oil)
5 tablespoons red wine vinegar
1/4 cup sour cream
2 tablespoons sugar
2 garlic cloves, crushed or minced
2 teaspoons chopped fresh parsley
1/2 teaspoon dry mustard
freshly ground pepper to taste

SALAD

2 (10- to 12-ounce) packages spinach, trimmed
4 hard-cooked eggs, finely chopped or shredded
8 slices bacon, crisp-cooked and crumbled
1 cup (4 ounces) shredded Swiss cheese croutons (optional)

For the dressing, combine the canola oil, vinegar, sour cream, sugar, garlic, parsley, dry mustard and pepper in a jar with a tight-fitting lid and seal tightly. Shake to mix. Chill for 6 hours or longer. You may store the dressing in the refrigerator for several weeks.

For the salad, mix the spinach, eggs, bacon, cheese and croutons in a salad bowl. Add the desired amount of dressing and toss to coat. Serve with crusty French bread. Leftover salad may be wilted and served warm the following day.

SPINACH AND STRAWBERRY SALAD

S E R V E S   6

POPPY SEED DRESSING

1/3 cup sugar
juice of 1 lemon
2 tablespoons wine vinegar
1 tablespoon vegetable oil
1 tablespoon mayonnaise
1 teaspoon poppy seeds

SALAD

1 (8-ounce) package baby spinach, trimmed
1 1/2 cups (8 ounces) sliced strawberries
1 small red onion, thinly sliced
1/2 cup sliced or chopped cucumber
1/4 cup (or more) sliced almonds, toasted

For the dressing, whisk the sugar, lemon juice, vinegar, oil, mayonnaise and poppy seeds in a bowl until mixed.

For the salad, toss the spinach, strawberries, onion, cucumber and almonds in a salad bowl. Add the dressing just before serving and toss to coat.

WARM WILTED SALAD
S E R V E S 2 T O 3

3 tablespoons olive oil
1/4 cup water
1 cup bite-size pieces green, yellow and
red bell pepper
1/3 cup broccoli florets
1/3 cup cauliflower florets
1 cup sliced celery cabbage
2/3 cup packaged broccoli slaw
1/2 cup shredded red cabbage
2 cups sliced romaine or mixed salad greens
1 cup baby spinach
salt to taste

Spray a skillet with nonstick cooking spray. Heat the olive oil and water in the prepared skillet over medium heat. Heat the bell pepper, broccoli and cauliflower in the olive oil mixture just until the vegetables begin to soften, stirring frequently. Add the celery cabbage, broccoli slaw, red cabbage, romaine and spinach to the vegetable mixture and toss. Heat just until barely wilted. Season with salt. When adding the vegetables to the skillet, begin with the vegetables with the firmest texture and end with the vegetables with the softest texture. All the vegetable ingredients in this recipe are optional; omit and add vegetable combinations as desired. You may serve as a warm side salad or top with grilled chicken breast, grilled salmon or sliced grilled beef for an entrée salad.

OLD-FASHIONED TOMATO ASPIC
S E R V E S 8

1 quart tomato juice
2 ribs celery, coarsely chopped
1 small onion, sliced
3 tablespoons sugar
2 tablespoons fresh lemon juice
1/2 bay leaf
1/2 teaspoon (scant) salt
1/8 to 1/4 teaspoon red pepper
2 1/2 tablespoons unflavored gelatin
1/2 cup cold water

Combine the tomato juice, celery, onion, sugar, lemon juice, bay leaf, salt and red pepper in a medium saucepan. Bring to a simmer, stirring occasionally. Simmer for 10 to 15 minutes, stirring occasionally.

Sprinkle the gelatin over the cold water in a large heatproof bowl. Let stand for 5 minutes or until softened. Strain the hot tomato juice mixture into the gelatin mixture and stir until the gelatin dissolves. Pour the tomato juice mixture into a 5-cup mold or into individual molds that have been rinsed with cold water. Chill until set. Serve with the Artichoke Mayonnaise on page 134.

FIRE AND ICE TOMATOES

SERVES 6 TO 8

6 large tomatoes, cut into quarters
1 onion, sliced and separated into rings
1 bell pepper, julienned
3/4 cup vinegar
1/4 cup cold water
1 1/2 teaspoons mustard seeds
1 1/2 teaspoons sugar
1 1/2 teaspoons celery salt
1/2 teaspoon salt
1/8 teaspoon red pepper
1/8 teaspoon black pepper

*T*oss the tomatoes, onion and bell pepper in a heatproof bowl. Combine the vinegar, cold water, mustard seeds, sugar, celery salt, salt, red pepper and black pepper in a saucepan and mix well. Bring to a boil. Boil for 1 minute, stirring occasionally. Pour the hot vinegar mixture over the tomato mixture and mix gently. Chill, covered, for several hours. You may store, covered, in the refrigerator for 2 to 3 days.

*S*arah Polk enjoyed remarkably good health throughout her life. On one occasion while living in the White House, however, she became gravely ill. President Polk became quite alarmed, writing in his diary that "I have never seen her suffer or complain more than she did for several hours after the chill subsided and the fever rose." Polk even moved his office temporarily to be near his ailing wife. Medical historians speculate that Sarah had contracted malaria, a common illness in the unhealthy city of Washington. Sarah managed to recuperate and outlive her illustrious husband by forty-two years, dying after a very brief illness at the age of eighty-seven.

Steeplechase Potato Salad

S E R V E S   6   T O   8

Seasoning Blend

1 tablespoon cracked black
peppercorns
1 tablespoon light brown sugar

1 teaspoon dill weed
1/2 teaspoon dry mustard
1/4 teaspoon salt

Salad

1 1/2 pounds unpeeled new potatoes
(about 10), cut into 3/4-inch pieces
4 hard-cooked eggs, separated
6 ounces andouille, cut into 1/4-inch
pieces (optional)
1/4 cup chopped shallots
1/4 cup minced yellow bell pepper
1/4 cup minced green bell pepper
1 tablespoon minced fresh gingerroot

1/2 cup water
1/4 cup white vinegar
1 1/2 teaspoons medium-hot pepper
sauce
1/4 cup mayonnaise
2 tablespoons cane vinegar or other
sweet vinegar
2 tablespoons cane syrup or molasses
1/4 cup chopped green onions

For the seasoning blend, mix the peppercorns, brown sugar, dill weed, dry mustard and salt in a bowl.

For the salad, combine the potatoes with enough water to cover in a saucepan. Bring to a boil. Boil for 20 minutes or just until tender; drain. Chop the egg whites. Set aside both the egg whites and yolks. Heat a heavy nonstick skillet over high heat for 3 to 4 minutes or until very hot. Cook the sausage in the hot skillet until brown around the edges, stirring frequently. Stir in the shallots, bell peppers and gingerroot. Cook for 3 to 4 minutes or until the bell peppers turn brown around the edges, stirring frequently. Stir in the seasoning blend, water, vinegar and pepper sauce. Cook for 4 to 5 minutes or until the vegetables are tender and the liquid is reduced, stirring frequently. Remove from the heat.

Strain the liquids from the skillet into a blender and place the sausage and vegetable mixture in a 2-quart salad bowl. Add the egg yolks, mayonnaise, cane vinegar and cane syrup 1 at a time to the blender, processing well after each addition. Add 1/2 cup of the potatoes, processing constantly until smooth and of a dressing consistency. Add the remaining potatoes to the vegetable mixture and mix gently. Stir in the egg whites and green onions. Add the dressing and toss gently. Serve warm or cold. The flavor of the salad is enhanced if prepared 1 day in advance and stored, covered, in the refrigerator.

COLD STEAK SALAD WITH CAPER VINAIGRETTE
SERVES 6

CAPER VINAIGRETTE
*1 cup extra-virgin olive oil
1/2 cup red wine vinegar or balsamic vinegar or
a combination of the two
3 tablespoons lemon juice
4 teaspoons drained capers
4 teaspoons Dijon mustard
3/4 teaspoon salt
1/4 teaspoon freshly ground pepper*

SALAD
*1 1/2 pounds boneless sirloin steak, 1 inch thick
12 ounces string beans, trimmed and blanched
8 ounces fresh mushrooms, sliced
2 tomatoes, peeled and cut into wedges
3/4 cup thinly sliced drained canned hearts of palm
1/2 red onion, thinly sliced and blanched
1 bunch watercress, trimmed
1 to 2 tablespoons chopped fresh oregano
1 to 2 tablespoons chopped fresh thyme
1 to 2 tablespoons chopped fresh basil*

For the vinaigrette, combine all the ingredients in a jar with a tight-fitting lid and seal tightly. Shake to mix.

For the salad, cook the steaks to the desired degree of doneness. Cut into 1-inch-thick slices and place the slices in a shallow nonreactive dish. Pour 1/3 of the vinaigrette over the slices and turn to coat. Marinate, covered, in the refrigerator for 1 to 3 hours, turning occasionally; drain. Combine the steak, beans, mushrooms, tomatoes, hearts of palm, onion and watercress in a salad bowl and mix gently. Add the desired amount of the vinaigrette and toss to coat. Sprinkle with the oregano, thyme and basil.

51

The Bible on which the President places his hand when taking the oath of office is an important icon of American democracy. Polk's inaugural Bible was presented to Sarah by the chief marshal of the District of Columbia. He inscribed the book to her, saying, "United with your distinguished husband and in the enjoinment of the utmost favor of his country and the highest station which their votes and their confidence can bestow, when time shall have passed and the troubles and the honors of this life shall have known their termination, may your union still continue undisturbed. . . ." Mrs. Polk cherished the book for the rest of her days.

TROPICAL CHICKEN SALAD
SERVES 8

DIJON DRESSING

1/2 cup sour cream   *1 tablespoon Dijon mustard*
1/2 cup mayonnaise   *salt and pepper to taste*

SALAD

3 cups (1-inch) chunks cooked   *1 cup chopped red onion*
chicken breasts   *1/3 cup raisins*
1 (8-ounce) can crushed pineapple,   *1/3 cup chopped dates*
drained   *sliced black olives (optional)*
1 cup chopped celery   *lettuce leaves*
1/2 cup chopped red bell pepper, or   *sliced strawberries or kiwifruit*
1 (2-ounce) jar chopped pimentos   *slivered almonds, toasted*

For the dressing, drain the sour cream in a colander for 15 minutes. Combine the drained sour cream, mayonnaise, Dijon mustard, salt and pepper in a bowl and mix well. Chill, covered, in the refrigerator.

For the salad, combine the chicken, pineapple, celery, bell pepper, onion, raisins, dates and olives in a bowl and mix well. Chill, covered, in the refrigerator. Add the desired amount of the dressing to the chicken mixture 1 to 2 hours before serving and toss to coat. Chill until serving time. Spoon the chicken salad onto lettuce-lined salad plates. Garnish with strawberries and/or kiwifruit. Sprinkle with almonds. You may prepare the ingredients 1 day in advance and store, covered, in the refrigerator, adding the dressing 1 to 2 hours before serving.

CALIFORNIA CHICKEN SALAD
S E R V E S   8   T O   1 0

CREAMY CURRY DRESSING

1/2 cup (1 stick) butter
2 cups mayonnaise
1/4 cup minced fresh parsley
1/2 teaspoon curry powder
1/4 teaspoon minced garlic
1/8 teaspoon marjoram
salt and pepper to taste

SALAD

4 cups shredded cooked chicken breasts
2 cups seedless grape halves
1/2 cup slivered almonds, toasted
lettuce leaves
paprika

For the dressing, melt the butter in a saucepan. Let stand until room temperature. Stir the butter gently into the mayonnaise in a bowl. Add the parsley, curry powder, garlic, marjoram, salt and pepper to the mayonnaise mixture and mix well. Store, covered, in the refrigerator.

For the salad, arrange the chicken, grapes and almonds on lettuce-lined salad plates. Top each serving with 2 tablespoons of the dressing and sprinkle with paprika. Serve immediately.

CHICKEN AND ARTICHOKE PASTA SALAD
S E R V E S   1 2

12 ounces rainbow rotini
chicken broth
3 cups shredded cooked chicken
1 (11-ounce) can diced tomatoes, drained
1 (8-ounce) can artichoke hearts, drained and chopped
8 ounces Parmesan cheese, shredded
1 (16-ounce) bottle Greek vinaigrette

Cook the pasta using package directions until al dente, substituting chicken broth for the water; drain. Toss the pasta, chicken, tomatoes, artichokes, cheese and vinaigrette in a large salad bowl until mixed. Chill, covered, until serving time.

PASTA LA BELLA RADIATORE
SERVES 6 TO 8

TARRAGON VINAIGRETTE

1 1/2 cups olive oil
1/2 cup tarragon vinegar
1 teaspoon Dijon mustard
3/4 teaspoon salt

1/2 teaspoon pepper
1/2 teaspoon garlic powder
1/4 teaspoon sugar

SALAD

16 ounces radiatore
2 cups chopped cooked chicken
8 ounces bacon, crisp-cooked and
crumbled
8 ounces Monterey Jack cheese,
shredded

6 ounces fresh spinach, julienned
1/2 cup sliced black olives
4 ounces Gorgonzola cheese,
crumbled

For the vinaigrette, combine the olive oil, vinegar, Dijon mustard, salt, pepper, garlic powder and sugar in a jar with a tight-fitting lid and seal tightly. Shake to mix.

For the salad, cook the pasta using package directions; drain. Toss the pasta, chicken, bacon, Monterey Jack cheese, spinach, olives and Gorgonzola cheese in a salad bowl. Add the vinaigrette and mix well.

For variety, substitute 1 pound coarsely chopped steamed fresh asparagus for the spinach. Or, omit the chicken and substitute orzo for the radiatore and serve as a side dish.

MALIBU SHRIMP AND PASTA SALAD

SERVES 8 TO 10

CELERY SEED DRESSING

1 cup vegetable oil
1/3 cup white vinegar
1/3 cup sugar
1/4 small onion, chopped
1 tablespoon celery seeds
1 teaspoon salt
1 teaspoon dry mustard

SALAD

16 ounces vermicelli, broken into 2-inch pieces
2 pounds medium shrimp, cooked,
peeled and deveined
2 cups finely chopped celery
2 (4-ounce) cans sliced black olives, drained
48 seedless green grapes, cut into halves
1 (8-ounce) jar finely diced pimentos, drained
1/2 cup chopped fresh parsley
6 tablespoons mayonnaise

For the dressing, combine the oil, vinegar, sugar, onion, celery seeds, salt and dry mustard in a jar with a tight-fitting lid and seal tightly. Shake to mix.

For the salad, cook the pasta using package directions. Drain and rinse with cold water. Combine the pasta, shrimp, celery, olives, grapes, pimentos and parsley in a bowl and mix gently. Add 1 cup of the dressing and toss to mix. Mix in the mayonnaise. Chill, covered, for 8 to 10 hours. Add the remaining dressing to the pasta salad just before serving and mix well.

After fourteen years in Washington as a U.S. congressman, James K. Polk returned to Tennessee in 1839 to run for governor. Although Sarah Polk did not accompany him on his political trips across the state, she played a crucial role in his campaign. She planned his schedule, answered or forwarded his mail, distributed campaign literature, consulted Democratic advisors, and sent letters to her husband with political news from Columbia and Nashville. The couple's teamwork brought success. James K. Polk narrowly defeated incumbent governor Newton Cannon in the election.

Marinated Shrimp and Tortellini Salad

SERVES 6 TO 8

Dijon Vinaigrette

3/4 cup olive oil
1/4 cup white wine vinegar
2 teaspoons Dijon mustard
2 teaspoons lemon juice
1 teaspoon salt

1/4 teaspoon sugar
1/4 teaspoon Greek seasoning
1/4 teaspoon ground black pepper
1/8 teaspoon cayenne pepper

Salad

1 (14-ounce) can artichoke hearts,
drained and cut into quarters
1 cup small fresh mushrooms
1 cup large pitted black olives
1 cup finely chopped red bell pepper

9 ounces cheese tortellini, cooked and
drained
8 to 16 ounces deveined peeled cooked
shrimp
1 tablespoon rinsed drained capers

For the vinaigrette, whisk the olive oil, vinegar, Dijon mustard, lemon juice, salt, sugar, Greek seasoning, black pepper and cayenne pepper in a bowl until mixed.

For the salad, toss the artichokes, mushrooms, olives, bell pepper, pasta, shrimp and capers in a large bowl until mixed. Add the vinaigrette and toss to coat. Chill for 3 hours or longer. Drain before serving.

ORZO SHRIMP SALAD

SERVES 6 TO 8

DILL DRESSING

1/4 cup plus 2 tablespoons chopped fresh dill weed
1 1/2 tablespoons chopped garlic
3 tablespoons olive oil
3 tablespoons lemon juice
1 1/2 tablespoons red wine vinegar
1/2 teaspoon salt
freshly ground pepper to taste

SALAD

2 pounds shrimp, cooked,
peeled and deveined
12 ounces orzo, cooked,
drained and rinsed
3 1/2 ounces feta cheese, crumbled
1 large tomato, chopped
red lettuce leaves

For the dressing, combine the dill weed, garlic, olive oil, lemon juice, vinegar, salt and pepper in a jar with a tight-fitting lid and seal tightly. Shake to mix.

For the salad, gently toss the shrimp, pasta, cheese and tomato in a large salad bowl until mixed. Add the dressing and toss to coat. Spoon the salad onto a platter lined with red lettuce. You may prepare 1 day in advance and store, covered, in the refrigerator. Double the recipe for a large crowd.

In the early 1800s, few congressmen brought their wives to Washington, D.C. Living quarters in the nation's capital were mostly overpriced or unsuitable for families. Sarah Polk relished the role of political wife, yet reluctantly stayed in Tennessee during her husband's first year in the House of Representatives. While living in a Washington boardinghouse with other legislators, James K. Polk received a letter from Andrew Jackson in Tennessee, who recounted a recent visit with Sarah: "She enjoys good health, but as you may expect complaining of your absence." The next year, Congressman Polk and his grateful wife rented rooms on Pennsylvania Avenue.

CARIBBEAN SEAFOOD SALAD

SERVES 4

1 avocado, chopped
2 tablespoons lime juice
1 1/2 pounds large fresh shrimp, peeled
  and deveined
1 pound fresh bay scallops
2 teaspoons minced garlic
1 tablespoon olive oil
1/2 cup lime juice

1/2 cup chopped fresh cilantro
1/4 cup honey
3 (15-ounce) cans black beans, drained
  and rinsed
1 purple onion, chopped
1 cup cooked whole kernel corn
baby lettuce leaves

*T*oss the avocado with 2 tablespoons lime juice in a bowl. Sauté the shrimp, scallops and garlic in the olive oil in a large skillet for 5 minutes or until the shrimp turn pink. Remove from the heat. Let stand until cool.

Whisk 1/2 cup lime juice, cilantro and honey in a large bowl until mixed. Add the avocado, shrimp mixture, beans, onion and corn to the honey mixture and toss to mix. Chill, covered, for 2 hours. Spoon the shrimp mixture onto 4 lettuce-lined serving plates. You may spread the shrimp mixture on a flour tortilla and roll tightly to enclose the filling, or stuff the shrimp mixture into a pita pocket.

BLEU CHEESE SALAD DRESSING

MAKES 1 QUART

*12 ounces bleu cheese or Roquefort
cheese, crumbled
2 cups mayonnaise
1 cup sour cream
1 small onion, grated
juice of 1 lemon*

Combine the cheese, mayonnaise, sour cream, onion and lemon juice in a mixing bowl. Beat until creamy, scraping the bowl occasionally. Store, covered, in the refrigerator.

HONEY MUSTARD SALAD DRESSING

MAKES 1 1/3 CUPS

*1/3 cup cider vinegar
1/3 cup Dijon mustard
1/3 cup honey
1/3 cup vegetable oil
salt to taste*

Combine the vinegar, Dijon mustard and honey in a bowl and mix well. Add the oil gradually, whisking constantly until blended. Season with salt. Decrease the amounts of the vinegar and Dijon mustard for a less tart dressing.

VINAIGRETTE AND VARIATIONS

MAKES 3/4 CUP

*1 medium shallot, finely chopped
2 tablespoons balsamic vinegar
1/2 teaspoon kosher salt
1/3 to 1/2 cup extra-virgin olive oil*

Combine the shallot, vinegar and kosher salt in a nonreactive bowl and mix well. Let stand for 30 minutes or until the salt dissolves. Whisk in the olive oil just before serving.

Follow these guidelines when preparing a vinaigrette. For a very acid vinaigrette, use 1 part oil to 1 part vinegar. For a medium acid vinaigrette, use 3 parts oil to 2 parts vinegar. For a mellow vinaigrette, use 3 parts oil to 1 part vinegar. The choices of vinegars are endless—red wine, white wine, tarragon, raspberry, cider, Champagne, balsamic, white balsamic—or substitute a little citrus juice for a portion of the vinegar. Oils can range from vegetable oil to canola oil to extra-virgin olive oil and walnut oil. Add pepper for sure. Try adding your favorite fresh or dried herbs, garlic or shallots or Hungarian paprika. For extras, try a little Dijon mustard and/or a bit of sugar or honey.

*This fan,
known as the
National Fan,
was presented
to Sarah Polk
by the President
at the time of
his inauguration.
The ornate
ivory and paper
fan features
portraits of all
of the presidents
from Washington
through the
newly elected
James K. Polk.*

Simply Soups

CREAM OF ARTICHOKE AND MUSHROOM SOUP

SERVES 4 TO 6

3/4 cup thinly sliced fresh mushrooms
2 tablespoons finely chopped onion
3 tablespoons butter
2 tablespoons flour
2 1/2 cups half-and-half
1 1/2 cups chicken broth
1 (16-ounce) can artichoke hearts, drained
and chopped
1/4 teaspoon thyme
salt and cayenne pepper to taste

Sauté the mushrooms and onion in the butter in a large saucepan for 5 minutes. Stir in the flour. Cook over low heat for 2 minutes, stirring constantly. Add the half-and-half and broth gradually, whisking constantly.

Cook over low heat until thickened, whisking constantly. Stir in the artichokes, thyme, salt and cayenne pepper. Cook just until heated through, stirring frequently. Ladle into soup bowls.

KAMA'AINA BEAN SOUP

SERVES 12

1 pound Polish sausage, sliced
4 cups water
2 (15-ounce) cans kidney beans
1 (8-ounce) can tomato sauce
3 medium potatoes, chopped
1 carrot, sliced
1/2 cup chopped onion
1 tablespoon salt
1 small head cabbage, chopped into
bite-size pieces
grated Parmesan cheese
pesto

Combine the sausage, water, undrained beans, tomato sauce, potatoes, carrot, onion and salt in a stockpot. Bring to a boil; reduce the heat. Simmer for 20 minutes, stirring occasionally. Stir in the cabbage.

Simmer for 20 minutes longer, stirring occasionally. Ladle into soup bowls. Top each serving with cheese and pesto.

ELEGANT MUSHROOM BISQUE

SERVES 4 TO 6

6 tablespoons butter
12 ounces mushrooms, thinly sliced
1 small onion, finely chopped
1 garlic clove, finely chopped
1 tablespoon lemon juice
2 1/4 cups chicken stock
2 2/3 cups milk
1 tablespoon flour
2/3 cup heavy cream
1 tablespoon chopped fresh chervil
1 tablespoon sherry
2 teaspoons finely chopped fresh parsley
salt and pepper to taste

Heat 3 tablespoons of the butter in a saucepan. Sauté 2 tablespoons of the mushrooms in the butter until tender. Remove the mushrooms to a platter using a slotted spoon, reserving the pan juices. Add the remaining 3 tablespoons butter to the reserved pan juices. Cook the remaining mushrooms, onion and garlic in the butter mixture until the mushrooms and onion are tender and the butter has been absorbed, stirring frequently. Stir in the lemon juice. Add the stock and mix well.

Cook, covered, over medium heat for 15 to 20 minutes, stirring occasionally. Process the mushroom mixture in a food processor until puréed. Return the purée to the saucepan. Whisk the milk and flour in a bowl until blended. Add the milk mixture to the purée and mix well. Cook until thickened, stirring constantly. Stir in the cream, chervil, sherry, parsley, salt and pepper. Ladle into soup bowls. Top each serving with some of the reserved sautéed mushrooms. For variety, garnish with sour cream or a wedge of puff pastry or sprinkle with chopped bacon or crumbled bleu cheese.

63

On the day of his inauguration James K. Polk was accompanied by his elegantly attired wife Sarah Polk to the U.S. Capitol. The two made a striking pair. Young and vibrant, they were a strong contrast to most of the first White House inhabitants. Mrs. Polk wore a stylish gown of blue satin. To occupy her hands she carried a gold fan that featured lithographic likenesses of all eleven Presidents, including her husband. On the reverse was a rendering of the signing of the Declaration of Independence. Known as the National Fan, it was to be treasured by Sarah Polk all her days.

ONION SOUP AU GRATIN

S E R V E S   4

―――

3 large sweet white onions, sliced
2 tablespoons butter
1 cup dry white wine
5 cups beef broth
1 bouquet garni (thyme, basil,
bay leaf, parsley)
cayenne pepper to taste
salt and black pepper to taste
1 cup (4 ounces) shredded Gruyère cheese or
Emmentaler cheese
4 thick slices French bread, toasted

―――

Brown the onions in the butter in a large saucepan over medium heat for 35 minutes, stirring frequently; do not allow to burn. Add the wine to the onion mixture and mix well. Cook over medium-high heat for 6 minutes, stirring frequently. Stir in the broth, bouquet garni, cayenne pepper, salt and black pepper.

Cook over medium heat for 30 minutes, stirring occasionally. Discard the bouquet garni. Spoon 2 tablespoons of the cheese into each of 4 ovenproof soup bowls. Ladle the soup into the prepared bowls. Top each serving with 1 bread slice and sprinkle with the remaining cheese. Arrange the bowls on a baking sheet. Broil for 8 minutes or until brown and bubbly. A preheated oven is recommended.

YELLOW PEPPER SOUP

S E R V E S   4   T O   6

―――

1 1/2 quarts chicken broth
4 yellow bell peppers, chopped
1 medium onion, chopped
1 fresh jalapeño chile, seeded and
cut into halves
8 ounces cream cheese, softened
1/2 teaspoon salt
1/4 teaspoon pepper
1/4 teaspoon curry powder

―――

Combine the broth, bell peppers, onion and jalapeño chile in a large saucepan. Bring to a simmer. Simmer for 20 to 25 minutes or until the bell peppers and onion are tender, stirring occasionally. Process the hot bell pepper mixture, cream cheese, salt, pepper and curry powder in a blender until puréed. Taste and adjust the seasonings. Chill, covered, in the refrigerator. Ladle into soup bowls. You may serve hot if preferred.

GOLDEN BUTTERNUT SQUASH SOUP

S E R V E S   8   T O   1 0

1 butternut squash
6 slices bacon, chopped
2 large yellow onions, chopped
1 1/2 tablespoons chopped fresh thyme, or
1 1/2 teaspoons dried thyme
5 1/4 cups (or more) chicken broth, vegetable broth or
reduced-sodium broth
1/3 cup heavy cream or half-and-half
3 tablespoons dry marsala or dry sherry
1/8 teaspoon cayenne pepper
salt and freshly ground black pepper to taste
fresh thyme leaves (optional)

Cut the squash horizontally into halves and remove the seeds and membranes. Arrange the squash cut side down in a baking pan. Add enough water to the pan to measure 1/4 inch. Bake at 375 degrees for 50 minutes or until tender. Let stand until cool. Scrape the pulp into a bowl; the pulp should measure 3 3/4 cups.

Sauté the bacon in a saucepan over medium heat until the fat is rendered. Stir in the onions and chopped thyme. Sauté for 8 minutes or until the onions are tender. Remove from the heat. Spoon the onion mixture into a food processor fitted with a metal blade or a blender. Process half the squash pulp at a time with the onion mixture until puréed. Return the purée to the saucepan. Stir in the broth.

Cook over medium-low heat for 20 minutes, stirring occasionally. Stir in the heavy cream, wine, cayenne pepper, salt and black pepper. Add additional broth if needed for a thinner consistency. Simmer just until heated through, stirring occasionally. Ladle into soup bowls and sprinkle with fresh thyme leaves. Add 1/8 teaspoon curry powder to the soup for variety. A preheated oven is recommended.

Sarah Polk's elegance and sophistication surprised Washington society. Few in the nation's capital expected such style from the wife of a populist frontier Democrat. Perhaps Sarah's impatience with the early-19th-century stereotype of the uncouth Westerner explains her curt response to a guest at one White House dinner. The guest tried to compliment the First Lady by remarking, "Madam, you have a very genteel assemblage tonight." Sarah replied, "I have never seen it otherwise."

CHICKEN FLORENTINE SOUP

SERVES 8

1 onion, chopped
1 teaspoon minced garlic
1/4 cup (1/2 stick) butter
1 (6-ounce) package small portobello
mushrooms, sliced
3 or 4 carrots, sliced
6 cups water
4 chicken bouillon cubes
4 boneless skinless chicken breasts,
cooked and chopped
1 (10-ounce) package frozen
spinach, thawed
1/2 teaspoon sage
1/2 teaspoon cayenne pepper
salt and black pepper to taste

Sauté the onion and garlic in half the butter in a skillet until the onion is tender. Remove the onion mixture to a bowl with a slotted spoon, reserving the pan juices. Heat the remaining butter with the reserved pan juices. Sauté the mushrooms in the butter mixture until tender.

Bring the water and bouillon to a boil in a saucepan. Parboil the carrots in the bouillon. Add the onion mixture, mushrooms, chicken, spinach, sage, cayenne pepper, salt and black pepper to the carrot mixture and mix well. Simmer for 1 hour, stirring occasionally. Ladle into soup bowls.

TURKEY TORTILLA SOUP

SERVES 8

1 large onion, chopped
1 tablespoon olive oil
1 (7-ounce) can chopped green chiles
2 large garlic cloves, chopped
1 teaspoon chili powder
1 teaspoon cumin
1/2 teaspoon oregano
1/4 teaspoon cayenne pepper
4 cups chicken broth
1 (14- to 16-ounce) can diced tomatoes
12 ounces cooked turkey, shredded
1 cup drained canned corn
1/3 cup fresh cilantro, chopped
salt and black pepper to taste
1 1/3 cups shredded Monterey Jack cheese
2 cups crushed tortilla chips

Sauté the onion in the olive oil in a 6-quart stockpot for 5 minutes. Stir in the green chiles, garlic, chili powder, cumin, oregano and cayenne pepper. Sauté for 1 minute. Add the broth and undrained tomatoes and mix well.

Bring just to a boil, stirring occasionally. Stir in the turkey; reduce the heat. Simmer for 3 minutes, stirring occasionally. Add the corn and cilantro and mix well. Season with salt and black pepper. Ladle into soup bowls. Top each serving with cheese and tortilla chips.

COLD WEATHER COMFORT SOUP

S E R V E S 1 0 T O 1 2

1¹/2 onions, chopped
1¹/2 carrots, cut into ¹/2-inch pieces
1¹/2 ribs celery, cut into ¹/2-inch pieces
1 red bell pepper, chopped
1 parsnip, cut into ¹/2-inch pieces
1¹/2 garlic cloves, chopped
¹/2 cup (1 stick) butter
1¹/2 teaspoons curry powder
1 bay leaf
¹/2 to ³/4 teaspoon cumin
¹/2 teaspoon salt
¹/4 teaspoon cinnamon
¹/4 teaspoon coriander
¹/4 teaspoon black pepper
¹/16 teaspoon allspice
¹/16 teaspoon cayenne pepper

6 cups (or more) chicken broth
1 (15-ounce) can peeled tomatoes,
  chopped
1¹/2 cups (or more) water
1¹/2 teaspoons tomato paste
3 pounds (or more) chicken breasts
  and thighs
¹/2 cup long grain rice
florets of ¹/2 head cauliflower
1 cup chopped broccoli or broccoli
  florets
8 ounces green beans, cut into
  1-inch pieces
1 small zucchini, chopped
1¹/2 pounds deveined peeled shrimp
chopped fresh parsley to taste

Sauté the onions, carrots, celery, bell pepper, parsnip and garlic in the butter in a stockpot until the vegetables are tender. Stir in the curry powder, bay leaf, cumin, salt, cinnamon, coriander, black pepper, allspice and cayenne pepper. Add the broth, undrained tomatoes, water and tomato paste and mix well. Bring to a boil. Add the chicken; reduce the heat.

Simmer for 1 hour, stirring occasionally. Remove the chicken to a platter using a slotted spoon. Discard the bay leaf. Chop the chicken, discarding the skin and bones. Set aside. Add the rice, cauliflower, broccoli, green beans and zucchini to the broth mixture and mix well.

Simmer for 15 to 20 minutes, stirring occasionally. Add the shrimp and chicken. Bring to a boil. Cook for 3 minutes or until the shrimp turn pink, stirring occasionally. Ladle into soup bowls and sprinkle with parsley. Serve with corn bread or crusty French bread.

MONDAY'S CHICKEN CHILI
S E R V E S 8

---

3 tablespoons extra-virgin olive oil
1 large onion, chopped
1 red bell pepper, chopped
1 green bell pepper, chopped
1 yellow bell pepper, chopped
1 jalapeño chile, seeded and minced
2 tablespoons minced garlic
2 tablespoons chili powder
1 teaspoon cumin
1/4 teaspoon coriander

1/4 teaspoon cinnamon
4 cups shredded cooked chicken
2 (28-ounce) cans Italian plum
* tomatoes, chopped*
1 (15-ounce) can dark red kidney
* beans, drained and rinsed*
1 tablespoon lemon juice
salt and pepper to taste
hot cooked rice or barley

Heat the olive oil in a large heavy stockpot. Cook the onion, bell peppers and jalapeño chile in the hot oil for 5 minutes, stirring frequently. Stir in the garlic. Cook until the vegetables are tender, stirring constantly. Mix the chili powder, cumin, coriander and cinnamon in a bowl. Add the spice mixture to the onion mixture and mix well. Cook until slightly fragrant, stirring constantly.

Combine the chicken, undrained tomatoes, beans and lemon juice in a bowl and mix well. Add the chicken mixture to the onion mixture and mix well. Season with salt and pepper. Simmer for 15 minutes, stirring occasionally. Ladle over hot cooked rice or barley in chili bowls. Serve with shredded cheese, sour cream and chopped scallions.

TOMATO SOUP WITH PESTO SWIRL

S E R V E S   4   T O   6

1/2 cup (1 stick) butter
2 tablespoons olive oil
1 large onion, sliced
2 1/2 pounds tomatoes, peeled
(about 6 or 7 tomatoes)
3 tablespoons tomato paste
3 3/4 cups chicken broth
1/4 cup flour
2 sprigs of fresh thyme, or
1/2 teaspoon dried thyme
4 fresh basil leaves, or
1/2 teaspoon dried basil
salt and pepper to taste
1 cup heavy cream
1/4 cup (1/2 stick) butter
1 teaspoon sugar
pesto

Heat 1/2 cup butter and olive oil in a saucepan until the butter melts. Cook the onion in the butter mixture until tender, stirring frequently. Add the tomatoes and tomato paste to the onion mixture and mix well. Simmer for 10 minutes, stirring occasionally. Add just enough of the broth to the flour in a bowl to moisten and mix well. Add the thyme, basil, salt and pepper to the flour mixture and mix well. Stir the flour mixture and remaining broth into the tomato mixture.

Simmer for 30 minutes, stirring occasionally. Let stand until cool. Process the tomato mixture in a blender until smooth. Return the tomato mixture to the saucepan and reheat over low heat. Stir in the heavy cream, 1/4 cup butter and sugar. Simmer just until heated through, stirring occasionally. Serve immediately or chill before serving. Swirl in a dollop of pesto before serving.

69

Concerned that the rigors of the Presidency were affecting James K. Polk's physical well-being, Sarah repeatedly urged her husband to leave his desk and accompany her on carriage rides through Washington. She admitted with frustration, "Somebody was always in the office, and Mr. Polk would not, or could not, come." The only thing that prompted the President to interrupt his work schedule was his concern about Sarah's health. When she was sick in bed in October 1847, he left a Cabinet meeting several times to visit her. During her recovery, he took her on a therapeutic carriage ride through the city.

DELTA DUCK GUMBO

SERVES 18

2 tablespoons flour	1¹/2 cups flour
3 cups water	1 green bell pepper, chopped
1 cup chopped celery	2 onions, chopped
1 large onion, chopped	1 cup chopped celery
1 apple, peeled and chopped	2 garlic pods, peeled and chopped
2 tablespoons Worcestershire sauce	1/4 cup (1/2 stick) butter
1 tablespoon lemon juice	1 tablespoon salt
1 tablespoon dry mustard	1 teaspoon black pepper
salt and black pepper to taste	1/2 teaspoon red pepper
4 ducks, dressed	1/2 teaspoon thyme
1 pound hot smoked sausage	1 tablespoon filé
1/2 cup vegetable oil	3 quarts water

Whisk 2 tablespoons flour into 3 cups water in a Dutch oven. Stir in 1 cup celery, 1 onion, apple, Worcestershire sauce, lemon juice, dry mustard and salt and black pepper to taste. Add the ducks and sausage. Bake, covered, at 350 degrees for 3 hours. Let stand until cool. Chop the duck, discarding the skin and bones. Chop the sausage. Return the chopped duck and sausage to the Dutch oven and mix well.

Heat the oil in a heavy skillet. Whisk in 1¹/2 cups flour until blended. Cook until the roux is dark brown, whisking constantly. Remove from the heat. Sauté the bell pepper, 2 onions, 1 cup celery and garlic in the butter in a heavy skillet until the vegetables are tender. Stir in 1 tablespoon salt, 1 teaspoon black pepper, red pepper and thyme.

Add the roux and sautéed vegetables to the duck mixture and mix well. Stir in the filé and 3 quarts water. Bring to a simmer. Simmer, covered, for 2 to 3 hours or to the desired consistency, stirring occasionally. Ladle into individual bowls. A preheated oven is recommended.

FIRE HALL BRUNSWICK STEW

S E R V E S   1 2

1 (3- to 4-pound) chicken
1 (28-ounce) can diced tomatoes
1 cup frozen lima beans
1 cup frozen Shoe Peg corn
1 large onion, chopped
2 large potatoes, peeled and chopped
1 tablespoon liquid smoke
8 ounces pulled barbecued pork
salt and pepper to taste

Combine the chicken with enough water to generously cover in a stockpot. Bring to a boil. Boil until tender. Remove the chicken to a platter, reserving the broth. Cool slightly. Chop the chicken, discarding the skin and bones.

Add the undrained tomatoes, beans, corn, onion, potatoes and liquid smoke to the reserved broth and mix well. Stir in the chicken and pork. Simmer until the vegetables are tender and the soup is the desired consistency, stirring occasionally and shredding the chicken as the soup simmers. Season with salt and pepper. Ladle into soup bowls.

MICROWAVE ROUX

M A K E S   2/3   C U P

2/3 cup vegetable oil
2/3 cup flour

Mix the oil and flour in a 4-cup microwave-safe measure. Microwave on High for 6 to 7 minutes, stirring at 6 minutes. The roux should be light brown at this stage. Microwave on High for 30 to 60 seconds longer or until dark brown. Use immediately or freeze for future use. Microwave times may vary. It should be noted that this roux recipe cannot be used to prepare the Delta Duck Gumbo recipe on page 70.

The dining room is the backdrop for some of the most beautiful presidential china ever made. The Polks had the President's seal embossed on all of the state china. Mrs. Polk also had different flowers and fruits painted on each piece.

Specialties of the House

JORDAN'S CAJUN BEEF BRISKET WITH BOURSIN CHEESE

SERVES 12 TO 15

BOURSIN

8 ounces cream cheese, softened	1 tablespoon marjoram
1/2 cup (1 stick) margarine, softened (do not use butter)	1 teaspoon garlic powder
	1 teaspoon sage

BASTING SAUCE

1 (10-ounce) can beef consommé	1 1/2 teaspoons dry mustard
1 1/2 cups water	1 teaspoon garlic powder
3/4 cup Worcestershire sauce	1 teaspoon hot sauce
1/3 cup cider vinegar	1 bay leaf
1/3 cup vegetable oil	1/2 teaspoon paprika

BRISKET AND ASSEMBLY

1/3 cup chili powder	1 (5- to 6-pound) beef brisket
2 tablespoons salt	hard rolls, split, or sliced French bread, toasted
1 1/2 tablespoons pepper	
1 tablespoon garlic powder	

For the cheese, combine the cream cheese, margarine, marjoram, garlic powder and sage in a bowl and mix well. Store, covered, in the refrigerator. Bring to room temperature before serving.

For the sauce, combine the consommé, water, Worcestershire sauce, vinegar, oil, dry mustard, garlic powder, hot sauce, bay leaf and paprika in a saucepan and mix well. Bring to a simmer, stirring occasionally. Remove from the heat.

For the brisket, mix the chili powder, salt, pepper and garlic powder in a bowl. Lightly coat the surface of the brisket with the chili powder mixture. Store any leftover spice mixture in a jar with a tight-fitting lid. Arrange the brisket fat side up in a shallow baking pan. Bake at 350 degrees for 1 hour; pour the basting sauce over brisket. Decrease the oven temperature to 250 degrees. Bake for 3 to 4 hours longer or to the desired degree of doneness, basting frequently with the sauce.

To serve, thinly slice the brisket. Spread the cheese on the cut sides of the rolls and arrange the rolls cut side up on serving plates. Arrange the beef over the rolls and drizzle with the pan juices. A preheated oven is recommended.

Northwest Saltimbocca of Beef with Bleu Cheese

S E R V E S 6

---

12 (2¹/2-ounce) beef tenderloin medallions
12 fresh sage leaves
6 thin slices prosciutto, cut into halves
¹/4 cup olive oil
8 ounces bleu cheese, crumbled
3 tablespoons minced shallots
1 tablespoon minced garlic
2 cups pinot noir
2 cups beef stock or broth
salt and pepper to taste

Arrange the medallions on a hard surface. Top each medallion with 1 sage leaf and 1 prosciutto half. Cover the layered medallions with plastic wrap. Pound ¹/4 inch thick with a meat mallet.

Heat the olive oil in a skillet over medium-high heat. Sear the medallions in the hot oil for 2 minutes per side. Remove the beef to a heated ovenproof platter using a slotted spoon, reserving the pan drippings. Sprinkle half the bleu cheese over the medallions and place the platter in a warm oven.

Sauté the shallots and garlic in the reserved pan drippings over medium heat until the garlic is golden brown. Deglaze the skillet with the wine. Stir in the stock and increase the heat to high. Cook until the sauce is reduced to ¹/3 of the original volume, stirring frequently. Remove from the heat. Whisk in the remaining bleu cheese. Season with salt and pepper.

To serve, arrange 2 medallions on each of 6 serving plates. Drizzle with the bleu cheese sauce. Serve immediately.

One of Mrs. Polk's legacies in the White House was the adoption of the song "Hail to the Chief" as the official Presidential anthem. A favorite of Sarah's, this song is included in a music book written in her own hand at age fourteen. As First Lady, she used the Scottish martial tune to help enhance her husband's presence in White House drawing rooms that were often filled with hundreds of guests who otherwise might not have noticed the average-size President enter.

FILET OF BEEF
S E R V E S   4   T O   6

1 (2- to 2 1/2-pound) beef filet
1 head garlic, separated into cloves
1/2 cup (1 stick) margarine
3 tablespoons wine vinegar
1 1/2 tablespoons Worcestershire sauce

*M*ake slits in the filet at 1 1/2-inch intervals and fill the slits with the garlic cloves. Arrange the filet in a baking pan.

Heat the margarine in a saucepan until melted. Stir in the vinegar and Worcestershire sauce. Bake the filet at 350 degrees for 40 minutes (no longer), basting frequently with the butter mixture. Let stand for 15 minutes before slicing into 1 1/2-inch medallions. A preheated oven is recommended.

VEAL MARSALA
S E R V E S   6

8 to 12 ounces fresh mushrooms, sliced
1 or 2 garlic cloves, crushed
1 tablespoon butter or olive oil
6 veal medallions
salt and pepper to taste
4 to 6 tablespoons flour
3 to 5 tablespoons butter
1/2 to 3/4 cup marsala, white wine or madeira
1 cup heavy cream

*S*auté the mushrooms and garlic in 1 tablespoon butter in a skillet until the mushrooms are tender. Remove the mushroom mixture to a bowl, reserving the pan juices. Season the veal with salt and pepper and lightly coat with the flour; make sure you coat with enough flour to thicken the sauce.

Add 3 to 5 tablespoons butter to the reserved pan juices and heat until the butter stops foaming. Sauté the veal in the butter until light brown. Remove the veal to a platter using a slotted spoon. Deglaze the skillet with the wine; the sauce will be dark. Stir in the cream.

Bring just to a boil. Return the mushrooms and veal to the skillet and mix well. Simmer for 2 minutes, stirring frequently. Serve immediately. You may substitute boneless skinless chicken breasts for the veal. Increase the cooking time by 10 to 15 minutes.

TEXAS-STYLE LASAGNA
SERVES 10 TO 12

1¹/2 pounds ground beef
1 (15-ounce) can tomato sauce
1 (14-ounce) can diced tomatoes
1 (4-ounce) can chopped green chiles
1 teaspoon seasoned salt
1 envelope taco seasoning mix
2 cups small curd cottage cheese
2 eggs, beaten
12 (6-inch) corn tortillas, torn
3¹/2 to 4 cups (14 to 16 ounces) shredded
Monterey Jack cheese

Brown the ground beef in a large skillet, stirring until crumbly; drain. Stir in the tomato sauce, undrained tomatoes, green chiles, seasoned salt and seasoning mix. Simmer for 15 to 20 minutes, stirring occasionally

Combine the cottage cheese and eggs in a bowl and mix well. Layer the ground beef mixture, tortillas, cottage cheese mixture and Monterey Jack cheese 1/2 at a time in a greased 9×13-inch baking dish.

Bake at 350 degrees for 30 minutes or until bubbly. Let stand for 10 minutes before serving. A preheated oven is recommended.

Sarah Polk shared her husband's belief that the White House should be accessible to the American people. Like earlier Presidents and First Ladies, the Polks hosted public receptions on New Year's Day and the Fourth of July. In his diary, President Polk described the open house on January 1, 1846: "All the halls, parlours and the East Room were crowded with visitors, ladies and gentlemen, and persons of all ages and sexes, without distinction of rank or condition in life." The Polks also scheduled public concerts by the Marine Band on the White House grounds and occasionally invited the audience into the reception rooms for refreshments.

BEEF STROGANOFF
S E R V E S   1 2

---

3 pounds filet of beef
6 tablespoons flour
salt and pepper to taste
1/2 cup (1 stick) butter
1/4 cup olive oil
1 pound fresh mushrooms, sliced
1 cup chopped onion
2 garlic cloves, crushed
1 cup sherry

1 cup beef bouillon
2 tablespoons Worcestershire sauce
1 teaspoon paprika
1/2 teaspoon tarragon, or to taste
2 cups sour cream
16 ounces flat egg noodles, cooked and drained
2 to 3 tablespoons butter, softened
1 teaspoon caraway seeds (optional)

Slice the beef into 2-inch strips. Mix the flour, salt and pepper in a shallow dish. Coat the beef strips with the flour mixture. Heat 1/2 cup butter and olive oil in a skillet until the butter melts. Cook the beef in the hot butter mixture until light brown on both sides; the beef should be rare. Remove the beef to a platter using a slotted spoon, reserving the pan drippings.

Sauté the mushrooms, onion and garlic in the reserved pan drippings over medium heat until the onion is tender and the liquid has been absorbed. Return the beef to the skillet. Stir in the sherry, bouillon, Worcestershire sauce, paprika, tarragon, salt and pepper.

Simmer for 5 minutes, stirring frequently. Stir in the sour cream. Simmer just until heated through, stirring frequently. Toss the hot noodles with 2 to 3 tablespoons butter and caraway seeds in a bowl. Serve with the stroganoff.

BEEF BURGERS FLORENTINE

S E R V E S   4

1 pound ground round
1¹/2 cups fresh spinach leaves, finely chopped
1 tablespoon soy sauce
1 tablespoon freshly ground pepper
1/2 teaspoon garlic salt
1 tablespoon olive oil
1/4 cup (1/2 stick) butter, softened
2 tablespoons grated Parmesan cheese
1 teaspoon chives
4 sesame seed hamburger buns, split and toasted

Combine the ground round, spinach, soy sauce and pepper in a bowl and mix well. Divide the ground round mixture into 4 equal portions. Shape each portion into a patty and sprinkle with garlic salt.

Heat the olive oil in a skillet over medium-high heat. Pan-broil the patties in the hot oil for 3 minutes and turn, draining pan drippings as needed. Continue cooking until the patties are cooked through; drain.

Mix the butter, cheese and chives in a bowl. Spread the butter mixture on the toasted sides of the buns and arrange 1 burger on each bun. Garnish as desired.

Did Sarah Polk host the White House's first Thanksgiving feast? Many historians think so. Although Thanksgiving Day did not become a national holiday until 1863, some states and cities (including Washington, D.C.) observed it earlier. A Washington newspaper noted that the Polks invited friends to dinner on Thanksgiving in 1846. If Sarah started a White House tradition, her husband seemed unaware of its significance. In his diary descriptions of Thanksgiving, President Polk wrote that he authorized the closing of public buildings and attended church, but never mentioned that he and his wife celebrated the holiday with a dinner.

ROASTED PORK TENDERLOIN WITH CORN BREAD CRUST

S E R V E S   4

1 (1-pound) pork tenderloin
2 teaspoons salt
1/2 teaspoon pepper
1 tablespoon olive oil
1 tablespoon unsalted butter

2 garlic cloves, minced
1 cup crumbled corn bread
1 teaspoon finely chopped fresh sage
salt and pepper to taste
2 tablespoons Dijon mustard

*P*at the tenderloin dry with paper towels and sprinkle with 2 teaspoons salt and 1/2 teaspoon pepper. Heat the olive oil in a nonstick skillet over high heat; do not allow to smoke. Sear the pork in the hot oil for 4 minutes or until brown on all sides, turning frequently. Remove the pork to a greased baking pan, reserving the pan drippings.

Heat the unsalted butter with the reserved pan drippings over medium heat. Sauté the garlic in the butter mixture for 30 seconds or until brown and fragrant. Remove from the heat. Stir in the corn bread crumbs, sage and salt and pepper to taste.

Coat the surface of the pork with the Dijon mustard. Pat half the crumb mixture over the mustard and then sprinkle with the remaining crumb mixture. Roast at 425 degrees for 20 to 25 minutes or until a meat thermometer registers 160 degrees. Check the pork after 15 minutes of roasting and cover loosely with foil if needed to prevent overbrowning. Let stand, loosely tented with foil, for 10 minutes before slicing. A preheated oven is recommended.

VOLUNTEER PORK TENDERLOIN

S E R V E S   8

---

2 (1-pound) pork tenderloins
1/2 cup each soy sauce and bourbon
1/2 cup packed brown sugar
1 cup orange marmalade, heated

Arrange the tenderloins in a shallow dish. Combine the soy sauce, bourbon and brown sugar in a bowl and mix well. Pour the soy sauce mixture over the tenderloins and turn to coat. Marinate, covered, in the refrigerator for 8 to 10 hours, turning occasionally; drain. Grill the tenderloins over medium heat until a meat thermometer registers 160 degrees, basting frequently with the marmalade. Let stand for 10 minutes before slicing.

GLAZED PORK LOIN

S E R V E S   4

1/3 cup each packed brown sugar and sugar
2 teaspoons salt
2 teaspoons dry mustard
1 (1-pound) pork loin or pork tenderloin

Combine the brown sugar, sugar, salt and dry mustard in a bowl and mix well. Line the bottom of a roasting pan with foil. Coat the pork with the desired amount of the brown sugar mixture and arrange the pork on a rack in the prepared roasting pan. Bake at 350 degrees for 30 minutes per pound or until a meat thermometer registers 160 degrees for medium. Let stand for 10 minutes before serving. A preheated oven is recommended.

Mindful of her husband's frugality with government funds, Sarah Polk skillfully balanced elegance and economy while planning White House dinners. Instead of employing a full-time chef, she hired caterer Auguste Julien, the son of Thomas Jefferson's chef, for part-time services. Following Sarah's instructions, steward Henry Bowman made special arrangements with prominent Washington shopkeepers, including a grocer, a baker, and a confectioner, who all offered large discounts in exchange for regular White House business. Sarah's only apparent extravagance was her insistence on serving expensive table wines instead of the cheap, potent whiskey punches that were popular in intemperate Washington society.

ANN'S ROASTED PORK CHOP DINNER
S E R V E S   4   T O   6

4 to 6 thick pork chops
salt and pepper to taste
2 onions, thinly sliced
6 tablespoons butter
1 cup chicken stock
1 cup white wine
1 bay leaf
peeled and sliced carrots
peeled potatoes, cut into quarters

Sprinkle the pork chops with salt and pepper. Brown the onions in the butter in a Dutch oven or electric skillet, stirring occasionally. Add the pork chops to the onion mixture. Cook until brown on both sides, turning occasionally. Add the stock, wine and bay leaf and mix well.

Simmer, covered, for 1 1/4 hours, stirring occasionally. Add carrots and potatoes and mix well. Simmer for 45 minutes longer or until the pork chops are cooked through and the vegetables are tender, stirring occasionally. Discard the bay leaf. Serve with baked apples.

OKTOBERFEST SAUSAGE SKILLET
S E R V E S   4

1 small onion, thinly sliced
3 tablespoons bacon drippings
1 (16-ounce) can sauerkraut,
drained and rinsed
1 medium apple, peeled and sliced
1/2 cup water
1 tablespoon sugar
1/2 teaspoon celery seeds
1/4 teaspoon salt
1/8 teaspoon pepper
1 pound smoked sausage or kielbasa,
cut into quarters

Sauté the onion in the bacon drippings in a skillet until tender. Stir in the sauerkraut, apple, water, sugar, celery seeds, salt and pepper. Cook, covered, over low heat for 15 minutes or until the apple is tender, stirring occasionally. Add the sausage to the apple mixture and mix well. Cook, covered, until the sausage is heated through, stirring occasionally.

GRILLED CHILI-MARINATED PORK TENDERLOIN

SERVES 6

1/4 cup fresh cilantro, chopped
1/4 cup lime juice
1/4 cup olive oil
1 tablespoon chili powder
1 tablespoon minced onion
2 teaspoons oregano
2 teaspoons minced garlic
1 teaspoon cumin
1/4 teaspoon cayenne pepper
2 pork tenderloins, cut crosswise into
1- to 11/2-inch slices

Combine the cilantro, lime juice, olive oil, chili powder, onion, oregano, garlic, cumin and cayenne pepper in a bowl and mix well. Pour over the pork in a shallow dish and turn to coat. Marinate, covered, in the refrigerator for 3 to 10 hours, turning occasionally. Grill over hot coals to the desired degree of doneness. You may use this marinade on chicken, turkey or beef.

Although Sarah Polk was popular and respected in Washington political circles, her strict Presbyterian scruples limited her social involvement. During her years as a congressman's wife, she refused to accompany friends to the horse races and the theater. As First Lady, she banned card playing and dancing in the White House. When a guest questioned the restrictions, Sarah replied, "To dance in these rooms would be undignified, and it would be respectful neither to the house nor to the office. How indecorous it would seem for dancing to be going on in one apartment, while in another we were conversing with dignitaries of the republic."

BUTTERFLIED LEG OF LAMB WITH CUCUMBER MINT SAUCE

S E R V E S   8   T O   1 0

LAMB

2 large garlic cloves, crushed
1/2 teaspoon salt
1/4 cup olive oil
2 tablespoons fresh lemon juice
1 tablespoon soy sauce

2 teaspoons coarsely ground pepper
1 (5 1/2- to 6-pound) leg of lamb, butterflied
1 tablespoon crushed rosemary

MINT SAUCE

1 cup sour cream or yogurt
1 cucumber, peeled, seeded and chopped
1 small onion, finely chopped

1/4 cup chopped fresh mint leaves
1 teaspoon minced garlic
salt and pepper to taste

For the lamb, mash the garlic and salt in a bowl until of a pasty consistency. Whisk in the olive oil, lemon juice, soy sauce and pepper. Rub the oil mixture over the surface of the lamb and coat with the rosemary. Arrange the lamb in a shallow dish. Marinate, covered, in the refrigerator for 2 to 10 hours.

Bring the lamb to room temperature. Grill over hot coals for 20 minutes or until a meat thermometer registers 145 degrees for medium-rare. Grill over hot coals for 40 minutes or until a meat thermometer registers 160 degrees for medium. Let stand for 15 minutes before serving.

For the sauce, combine the sour cream, cucumber, onion, mint, garlic, salt and pepper in a bowl and mix well. Serve the sauce with the lamb along with pita bread.

NANCY KEY'S LAMB CURRY

S E R V E S   1 0   T O   1 2

5 to 6 pounds boneless lamb, cut into 1 1/2-inch cubes
1/2 cup flour
1/2 cup vegetable oil
12 ounces carrots, sliced
3 cups chopped onions
2 cups chopped celery
8 cups chicken broth
6 bananas, cut into chunks
4 large tart apples, peeled and cut into 1/2-inch pieces
1 1/3 cups sweetened coconut
1 cup raisins
1 cup chutney
4 bay leaves
8 to 10 tablespoons hot curry powder
7 tablespoons tomato paste
1 teaspoon thyme
1/2 teaspoon minced garlic
1 cup heavy cream (optional)
hot cooked rice

Coat the lamb with the flour. Brown the lamb on all sides in the oil in a stockpot. Add the carrots, onions and celery and mix well. Cook until the onions are tender, stirring frequently. Stir in the broth, bananas, apples, coconut, raisins, chutney, bay leaves, curry powder, tomato paste, thyme and garlic and mix well. Bring to a boil; reduce the heat.

Simmer, covered, over low heat for 1 1/2 hours, stirring occasionally. Discard the bay leaves. Add the cream if desired to tone down the spices and mix well. Simmer just until heated through. Serve over hot cooked rice.

White House life in the early 19th century offered little privacy or security. Sarah Polk's visiting niece Joanna Rucker described the situation: "The house belongs to the Government and everyone feels at home and they sometimes stalk into our bedroom and say they are looking at the house." Conscious of her obligations as First Lady, Sarah was charming and courteous to her expected and unexpected guests. In the spring of 1845, however, an unwelcome visitor tested her composure. A stranger entered the White House and ran from room to room waving a knife until he was finally subdued in Sarah's private parlor.

ROASTED LAMB RIBLETS

S E R V E S   6

1/4 cup chopped fresh parsley
3 garlic cloves, minced
2 tablespoons minced fresh rosemary
1 teaspoon minced fresh thyme
1/2 cup Dijon mustard
1 1/2 tablespoons kosher salt
1 1/2 tablespoons balsamic vinegar
pepper to taste
2 racks of lamb
cornmeal

Process the parsley, garlic, rosemary and thyme in a small food processor until combined or combine the herbs using a mortar and pestle. Add the Dijon mustard, salt, vinegar and pepper to the herb mixture. Process for 1 minute or until blended.

Arrange the lamb racks with the ribs curving down on an oiled broiler rack in a broiler pan. Coat the tops with the mustard mixture and sprinkle the entire surface with cornmeal to form a crust. Roast at 450 degrees for 20 minutes for rare or for 25 minutes for medium-rare. Let stand, tented with foil, for 15 minutes before cutting into individual riblets. A preheated oven is recommended.

REUBEN CASSEROLE

S E R V E S   6

1 (27-ounce) can sauerkraut,
drained and rinsed
1 cup sour cream
1 medium onion, minced
1 1/2 pounds corned beef, chopped, or
1 (24-ounce) can corned beef
4 cups (16 ounces) shredded Swiss cheese
10 slices dark rye bread, crumbled or cubed
1 cup (2 sticks) margarine, melted

Combine the sauerkraut, sour cream and onion in a bowl and mix well. Spread the sauerkraut mixture in a buttered 9×13-inch baking pan. Crumble the corned beef over the prepared layer. Sprinkle the cheese and bread crumbs over the prepared layers and drizzle with the margarine. Bake at 350 degrees for 45 minutes. A preheated oven is recommended.

TURKEY REUBEN BAKE

S E R V E S 6

1 (16-ounce) can sauerkraut,
drained and rinsed
2 cups (bite-size pieces) cooked turkey
2 cups (8 ounces) shredded Swiss cheese
1/2 cup mayonnaise
1/4 cup Thousand Island salad dressing
3 medium tomatoes, sliced
6 slices dark pumpernickel bread,
cut into cubes
3 tablespoons butter, melted

Layer the sauerkraut, turkey and cheese in the order listed in a greased 7×11-inch baking dish. Mix the mayonnaise and salad dressing in a bowl and spread the mayonnaise mixture over the prepared layers. Top with the tomatoes and bread cubes and drizzle with the butter. Bake at 350 degrees for 35 to 45 minutes or until brown and bubbly. A preheated oven is recommended.

A few critics thought that Sarah Polk's strict Presbyterian rectitude seemed excessive, but no one questioned the sincerity of her faith. Despite her firm beliefs and her regular worship attendance, she did not join a church until age thirty, when she finally felt adequately prepared. As First Lady, she occasionally invited guests to sing hymns with her at the White House piano. Her piety did not preclude a fondness for some worldly pleasures such as fashion. She attracted considerable attention one Sunday when she entered church late wearing a shimmering black silk coat and a wide-brim hat with a large ostrich plume.

SOUTH-OF-THE-BORDER CHICKEN
S E R V E S   4   T O   6

*4 boneless skinless chicken breasts,
cut into 1-inch pieces
salt and pepper to taste
3 tablespoons canola oil
1 1/2 cups chopped onions
1 green bell pepper, chopped
2 garlic cloves, minced
1 (28-ounce) can diced tomatoes
1/3 cup raisins
1/4 cup dry sherry (optional)
2 teaspoons chili powder
1/4 teaspoon ground cloves
1/3 cup sliced green olives or black olives
hot cooked yellow rice*

Sprinkle the chicken with salt and pepper. Heat the canola oil in a large saucepan over medium-high heat. Sauté the chicken in the hot oil until brown on all sides. Remove the chicken to a platter, reserving the pan drippings. Reduce the heat to medium.

Sauté the onions, bell pepper and garlic in the reserved pan drippings for 3 to 4 minutes or until the onions are tender. Stir in the chicken, undrained tomatoes, raisins, sherry, chili powder and cloves. Reduce the heat to low.

Simmer, covered, for 30 to 40 minutes or until the chicken is cooked through and the mixture is the desired consistency, stirring occasionally. Stir in the olives just before serving. Spoon over hot cooked yellow rice. Serve with a green salad.

CHICKEN SARAHBELLA
S E R V E S   8

*2 1/2 pounds chicken breasts
1/2 cup each red wine vinegar and olive oil
1/4 cup dried oregano
1 head garlic, peeled and puréed
6 bay leaves
coarse salt and ground pepper to taste
1 cup pitted prunes
1/2 cup pitted Spanish green olives
1/2 cup drained capers
1 cup packed brown sugar
1 cup white wine
1/4 cup chopped fresh parsley*

Arrange the chicken in a shallow dish. Mix the vinegar, olive oil, oregano, garlic, bay leaves, salt and pepper in a bowl. Stir in the prunes, olives and capers. Pour the vinegar mixture over the chicken and turn to coat. Marinate, covered, in the refrigerator for 8 to 10 hours, turning occasionally.

Transfer the chicken mixture to a 9×13-inch baking pan. Sprinkle with the brown sugar and drizzle with the wine. Bake at 350 degrees for 50 to 60 minutes or until the chicken is cooked through, basting with the pan juices frequently. Discard the bay leaves.

Remove the chicken to a platter using a slotted spoon. Top with the prunes, olives and capers and drizzle with some of the pan juices. Sprinkle with the parsley. Serve hot or cold with the remaining pan juices. A preheated oven is recommended.

MEXICAN FIESTA CHICKEN PLATTER

SERVES 3 TO 6

2 (or more) eggs
1 (8- to 16-ounce) bottle medium-hot salsa
1/4 teaspoon salt
1 cup fine dry bread crumbs
1 teaspoon chili powder
1 teaspoon cumin
3/4 teaspoon garlic salt
3/4 teaspoon crushed oregano
6 boneless skinless chicken breasts
1/4 cup (1/2 stick) butter or margarine
4 to 6 cups shredded iceberg lettuce
1 to 2 cups sour cream
4 to 6 scallions with tops, thinly sliced
1 ripe avocado, thinly sliced
12 to 18 cherry tomatoes, cut into halves
1 lime, cut into thin wedges

Whisk the eggs in a bowl until blended. Stir in 3 tablespoons of the salsa and the salt. Mix the bread crumbs, chili powder, cumin, garlic salt and oregano in a shallow dish. Dip each chicken breast in the egg mixture and coat with the crumb mixture.

Heat the butter in a baking pan in a 350-degree oven until melted. Arrange the chicken in a single layer in the prepared pan, turning to coat each piece with butter. Bake at 350 degrees for 25 minutes or until cooked through.

Arrange the chicken on a lettuce-lined serving platter. Top each chicken breast with a dollop of the sour cream. Arrange the scallions, avocado slices, cherry tomatoes and lime wedges around the chicken. Pass the remaining sour cream and remaining salsa with the chicken. Serve with corn pudding or seasoned rice. A preheated oven is recommended.

The eighty-eight years of Sarah Childress Polk's life saw amazing changes in the ways people communicated. As a young girl growing up on the Western frontier, she was obliged to write letters to friends and family who lived any distance from her. When her husband received the nomination for the Presidency at the 1844 Democratic National Convention in Baltimore, the new invention of the telegraph immediately sent the news to Washington, D.C. Yet in 1877, the seventy-four-year-old Sarah Polk was given the honor of receiving the very first telephone in Nashville.

CHICKEN QUESADILLAS
S E R V E S   5   T O   6

6 boneless skinless chicken breasts
1/2 cup vegetable oil
juice of 2 limes
2 garlic cloves, minced
1 to 2 teaspoons cayenne pepper
1/8 teaspoon hot sauce
salt and black pepper to taste
3 to 4 tablespoons vegetable oil
1 green bell pepper, sliced

1 red bell pepper, sliced
1 yellow bell pepper, sliced
1 onion, sliced
10 to 12 flour tortillas
2 cups (8 ounces) shredded Cheddar
cheese or Monterey Jack cheese
salsa
guacamole

Place the chicken in a sealable plastic bag. Mix 1/2 cup oil, lime juice, garlic, cayenne pepper, hot sauce, salt and black pepper in a bowl. Pour the oil mixture over the chicken and seal tightly. Turn to coat. Marinate in the refrigerator for 6 to 8 hours, turning occasionally; drain. Grill the chicken over hot coals until cooked through, turning occasionally. Cool slightly and cut into strips.

Heat 3 to 4 tablespoons oil in a small skillet. Sauté the bell peppers and onion in the hot oil until tender. Heat 1/2 teaspoon of the 3 to 4 tablespoons oil in a skillet over medium-high heat. Place 1 tortilla in the hot skillet. Layer the chicken, bell pepper mixture and cheese on half the tortilla and fold over to enclose the filling; flatten lightly with a spatula. Cook until the cheese melts and the tortilla is light brown, turning once. Repeat the process with the remaining oil, remaining tortillas, remaining chicken, remaining bell pepper mixture and remaining cheese. Serve with salsa and guacamole.

GRILLED MARINATED LIME CHICKEN

S E R V E S 6

---

6 small whole chicken breasts
1/2 cup packed brown sugar
1/4 cup cider vinegar
juice of 1 lime
juice of 1/2 large lemon
3 tablespoons sweet coarse grain mustard
1 1/2 teaspoons salt
3 medium garlic cloves, crushed
6 tablespoons olive oil
pepper to taste
watercress and/or endive (optional)

Arrange the chicken in a shallow nonreactive dish. Mix the brown sugar, vinegar, lime juice, lemon juice, mustard, salt and garlic in a bowl. Whisk in the olive oil and pepper.

Pour the lime mixture over the chicken and turn to coat. Marinate, covered, in the refrigerator for 8 to 10 hours, turning once; drain. Let stand at room temperature for 15 to 30 minutes. Grill the chicken over hot coals until cooked through, turning once. Garnish with watercress and/or endive. You may broil the chicken if desired.

During her long widowhood, Sarah Polk was visited by many dignitaries who hoped to meet the former First Lady. During the Civil War, she was visited by both Confederate and Union commanders. The Tennessee State Legislature always called in a body on New Year's Day to pay their respects. At least two U.S. Presidents came to call. President and Mrs. Rutherford B. Hayes came to Polk Place in 1877. Like Sarah, Lucy Hayes curbed drinking while in the White House. In 1887, President Cleveland visited Mrs. Polk. They spoke about events in Washington and, according to Mrs. Polk, "built and rebuilt the White House."

JULIA'S CHICKEN CASSEROLE

SERVES 8 TO 10

2 (6-ounce) packages long grain and wild rice mix
2 (8-ounce) cans sliced water chestnuts, drained
2 medium onions, chopped
4 ribs celery, chopped
1/4 cup (1/2 stick) butter or margarine
6 cups chopped cooked chicken
12 ounces Cheddar cheese, shredded
2 cups sour cream
1 (10-ounce) can cream of mushroom soup
1 (10-ounce) can cream of celery soup
1 cup milk
salt and pepper to taste
bread crumbs
4 ounces Cheddar cheese, shredded

Cook the rice using package directions. Sauté the water chestnuts, onions and celery in the butter in a large skillet for 10 minutes or until tender. Stir in the rice, chicken, 12 ounces cheese, sour cream, soups, milk, salt and pepper.

Spoon the chicken mixture into a greased 10×15-inch baking dish. Sprinkle with bread crumbs. Bake at 350 degrees for 30 minutes. Sprinkle with 4 ounces cheese. Bake for 5 minutes longer. A preheated oven is recommended.

LOW-FAT CHICKEN LASAGNA

SERVES 6 TO 8

3 cups chopped cooked chicken
1 (10-ounce) can reduced-fat and -sodium cream of mushroom soup
1 cup fat-free cottage cheese
1/2 cup plain yogurt
1/3 to 1/2 cup chopped onion
1/3 cup grated Parmesan cheese
2 eggs, beaten
1/4 teaspoon garlic powder
seasoned salt to taste
1 (10-ounce) package frozen chopped broccoli, thawed
9 lasagna noodles, cooked and drained
9 slices low-fat American cheese, cut into strips
shredded Cheddar cheese
paprika to taste

Combine the first 9 ingredients in a bowl and mix well. Stir in the broccoli. Spread 1/4 of the chicken mixture in a 7×11-inch baking dish sprayed with nonstick cooking spray. Arrange 3 of the noodles over the prepared layer. Spread with 1/3 of the remaining chicken mixture and top with 1/3 of the American cheese strips.

Repeat the layering process 2 more times with the remaining chicken mixture, noodles and American cheese. Sprinkle with shredded Cheddar cheese and paprika. Bake, covered with foil, at 350 degrees for 45 minutes or until bubbly. Let stand for 5 minutes before serving. A preheated oven is recommended.

THE CHICKEN CURRY EVENT

S E R V E S 6

1/2 cup unbleached flour
salt and freshly ground pepper to taste
3 whole chicken breasts, boned and split
5 tablespoons unsalted butter
1 onion, minced
2 green bell peppers, chopped
3 garlic cloves, minced
3 tablespoons (or more) curry powder
1 (15-ounce) can stewed tomatoes
1 (15-ounce) can cream of coconut
Tabasco sauce to taste
Worcestershire sauce to taste
1 cup currants or raisins

Mix the flour with salt and pepper in a shallow dish. Coat the chicken with the seasoned flour mixture. Brown the chicken lightly on both sides in 3 tablespoons of the unsalted butter in a skillet. Remove the chicken to a baking dish using a slotted spoon, reserving the pan drippings.

Heat the remaining 2 tablespoons unsalted butter with the reserved pan drippings. Sauté the onion, bell peppers and garlic in the butter mixture until the onion is tender. Stir in the curry powder. Cook for 1 minute, stirring frequently. Stir in the undrained tomatoes and cream of coconut.

Bring to a simmer, stirring frequently. Season with Tabasco sauce and Worcestershire sauce. Stir in the currants. Spoon the curry mixture over the chicken. Bake, covered, at 350 degrees for 45 minutes or until the chicken is cooked through. Serve with hot cooked rice and/or cashews, banana chips, chopped apples, mango chutney, toasted coconut, chopped scallions or condiments of choice. A preheated oven is recommended.

The Civil War was a particularly difficult time for Sarah Polk, living in Nashville. Sarah remained publicly neutral during the war. As Nashville changed hands from a Confederate-held city to a Union stronghold early in the war, she was visited by commanders from both sides. She was a member of a Confederate relief organization that made clothing and bandages for soldiers. At the same time, she became good friends with Union General Thomas and his wife. Because of her neutrality, she became the keeper and guardian of the collections of the Tennessee Historical Society.

SZECHWAN CHICKEN STIR-FRY
SERVES 4

3 tablespoons soy sauce
1 tablespoon cornstarch
2 large boneless skinless chicken
breasts, cut into 1/2-inch pieces
1 tablespoon dry sherry
2 teaspoons sugar
1 teaspoon white vinegar
1/4 cup vegetable oil
(do not use olive oil)
1 teaspoon crushed red pepper flakes
2 scallions, sliced

1/2 teaspoon ginger
1/2 cup salted peanuts or cashews
1/2 cup vegetable oil (do not use
olive oil)
8 ounces fresh mushrooms, sliced
1 (8-ounce) can water chestnuts or
bamboo shoots, drained
1 pound fresh spinach, stems removed
2 teaspoons sugar
1/2 teaspoon salt
hot cooked basmati rice

*M*ix 1 tablespoon of the soy sauce and the cornstarch in a bowl. Add the chicken and toss to coat. Combine the remaining 2 tablespoons soy sauce, sherry, 2 teaspoons sugar and vinegar in a bowl and mix well.

Heat 1/4 cup oil in a large skillet or wok. Stir in the red pepper flakes. Cook until dark. Add the chicken and mix well. Cook for 2 minutes, stirring constantly. Remove the chicken to a platter using a slotted spoon, reserving the pan drippings. Stir-fry the scallions and ginger in the reserved pan drippings for 1 minute. Return the chicken to the skillet. Stir-fry for 2 minutes. Stir in the sherry mixture and peanuts. Stir-fry for 1 minute longer. Remove the chicken mixture to a bowl. Cover to keep warm.

Heat 1/2 cup oil in the skillet over medium-high heat. Sauté the mushrooms quickly. Add the water chestnuts. Stir-fry for 2 minutes. Add the spinach. Stir-fry for 1 minute or until wilted. Stir in 2 teaspoons sugar and salt. Stir-fry for 2 minutes. Stir in the chicken mixture. Stir-fry just until heated through. Using a slotted spoon, spoon the chicken mixture over hot cooked rice on serving plates.

SEVENTH STREET CHICKEN

S E R V E S   6

1 1/2 to 2 pounds boneless skinless chicken breasts
1 rib celery
1 tablespoon Italian seasoning
salt and pepper to taste
1 (8-ounce) package corn bread stuffing mix
1/2 cup (1 stick) margarine, melted
1 (10-ounce) can cream of chicken soup
1 (10-ounce) can cream of celery soup
1/4 cup mayonnaise
2 soup cans water

Combine the chicken, celery, Italian seasoning, salt and pepper with enough water to cover in a stockpot. Bring to a boil; reduce the heat. Cook for 45 minutes or until the chicken is cooked through; drain. Chop the chicken into bite-size pieces. Combine the stuffing mix and margarine in a bowl and mix well. Mix the soups, mayonnaise and 1/2 soup can water in a bowl until blended.

Layer 1/2 of the stuffing mixture, 1/2 of the chicken and 1/2 of the soup mixture in a greased 9×13-inch baking dish. Pour 1/2 soup can water over the layers. Top with the remaining stuffing mixture, remaining chicken and remaining soup mixture. Pour the remaining 1 soup can water over the prepared layers. Bake, covered with foil, at 350 degrees for 45 minutes; remove the foil. Bake for 15 minutes longer. The amount of water may be adjusted according to taste, adding less water for a drier consistency and additional water for a creamier consistency. A preheated oven is recommended.

Polk Place in Nashville was the final home of James and Sarah Polk. It was originally dubbed Grundy Place after the first owner, Felix Grundy, who happened to be Polk's law mentor. After Grundy's death in 1840, Polk began purchasing his property in Nashville. Polk immediately began updating the Palladian-style home to the modern Greek Revival. While in Washington, the Polks purchased furnishings for the home. Looking forward to a long retirement, James K. Polk died at Polk Place just fifty-two days after moving in. Sarah lived there forty-two years beyond him, making the home something of a shrine to her deceased husband.

BIGBY CREEK VENISON
SERVES 6 TO 8

1 (3- to 4-pound) venison roast or
venison pieces, trimmed
1/2 cup white vinegar
2 tablespoons salt
6 garlic cloves, chopped
1 teaspoon salt
flour
2 to 3 tablespoons vegetable oil

1 large onion, sliced
1 (14-ounce) can diced tomatoes
1/3 cup white vinegar
3 tablespoons brown sugar
3 tablespoons Worcestershire sauce
3 garlic cloves, chopped
1 1/2 teaspoons dry mustard

Place the venison in a large deep bowl. Mix 1/2 cup vinegar, 2 tablespoons salt and 6 chopped garlic cloves in a bowl. Pour the vinegar mixture over the venison. Add enough water to the bowl to cover the venison. Marinate, covered with plastic wrap, in the refrigerator for 8 to 10 hours.

Drain the venison and pat dry, discarding the marinade. Sprinkle with 1 teaspoon salt and coat with flour. Sauté the venison in the oil in a heavy skillet until brown on all sides. Remove the venison to a slow cooker and top with the onion.

Mix the undrained tomatoes, 1/3 cup vinegar, brown sugar, Worcestershire sauce, 3 chopped garlic cloves and dry mustard in a bowl. Pour the tomato mixture over the venison. Cook, covered, on Low for 8 to 10 hours, stirring occasionally. Serve over hot cooked noodles with a green salad and crusty French bread.

TENNESSEE RIVER DUCK AND DRESSING

SERVES 10 TO 12

CORN BREAD
2 tablespoons melted bacon drippings
2 cups cornmeal
1 1/2 teaspoons salt
1 teaspoon baking soda
2 cups buttermilk
2 eggs

DUCKS
4 ducks, dressed
2 cups chopped onions
2 cups chopped celery
1/2 can Cavender's Greek seasoning
2 teaspoons sage
salt and pepper to taste
2 (14-ounce) cans chicken broth

For the corn bread, heat the bacon drippings in a cast-iron skillet in a 450-degree oven until smoking. Combine the cornmeal, salt and baking soda in a bowl and mix well. Add the buttermilk and eggs and mix well. Spoon the batter into the hot skillet. Bake for 15 to 20 minutes or until brown. Cool slightly and crumble the corn bread into a large bowl. Decrease the oven temperature to 350 degrees.

For the ducks, combine the ducks with enough water to cover in a stockpot. Boil until the ducks are tender; drain. Let stand until cool. Chop the duck, discarding the skin and bones. Add the duck, onions, celery, Greek seasoning, sage, salt and pepper to the corn bread and toss to mix. Add the broth and mix well. Spoon the duck mixture into a 3-quart baking dish. Bake at 350 degrees for 1 1/2 hours or until light brown. A preheated oven is recommended.

One of the best ways of understanding people from the past is to read what their contemporaries thought of them. Many wrote about Mrs. Polk. Future President Franklin Pierce said that he preferred to talk politics with Sarah over anyone else, including President Polk himself. Vice President George Dallas thought that Mrs. Polk was "master of herself, and I suspect of somebody else also." Yet another contemporary thought Sarah had "both sagacity and decision" that would make her a good counselor in some emergencies. Even Senator Sumner, known as a dour man, remarked that "Sarah's sweetness of manner won me entirely."

BARBECUED DOVE

S E R V E S   4

---

8 dove
1/2 to 1 cup (1 to 2 sticks) unsalted
butter, clarified

Grill the dove over high heat just until brown on all sides; decrease the heat. Place the dove in a disposable aluminum pan. Pour the clarified butter over the dove and cover with foil.

Arrange the pan on the grill rack. Grill, with the lid closed, over low heat for 1½ hours. If desired sear the dove in a skillet and bake, covered, at 250 degrees for 1½ hours.

To clarify butter, heat the butter in a saucepan over low heat until melted; skim the top. Let stand for several minutes to allow the milk solids to sink to the bottom of the pan. The clarified butter is then poured off to be used in cooking. A preheated oven is recommended.

QUAIL STUFFED WITH OYSTERS

V A R I A B L E

---

quail, dressed
salt and pepper to taste
2 or 3 fresh oysters per quail
melted butter
cornmeal
softened butter
flour
1 slice bacon per quail

Rub the quail with salt and pepper inside and out. Dip the oysters in melted butter and coat with cornmeal. Stuff the oysters into the quail. Arrange the quail in a baking pan.

Mix softened butter with just enough flour in a bowl to make a pasty consistency. Brush the butter mixture over the quail and top with the bacon. Bake at 375 degrees for 1 hour or until the quail are cooked through and crisp. Broil until brown if desired. A preheated oven is recommended.

SMOTHERED QUAIL OR DOVE

SERVES 10 TO 12

1 cup chopped green onions
2 slices bacon, chopped
2 garlic cloves, finely chopped
chopped mushrooms to taste
1/2 cup (1 stick) butter
24 quail breasts or dove breasts
salt and pepper to taste
3 tablespoons flour
2 cups chicken stock
1 cup sherry or white wine
1/2 teaspoon tarragon

Sauté the green onions, bacon, garlic and mushrooms in the butter in a skillet until the bacon is brown. Remove the bacon mixture to a bowl using a slotted spoon, reserving the pan drippings.

Sprinkle the quail with salt and pepper. Sear on both sides in the reserved pan drippings. Remove the quail to a baking dish using a slotted spoon, reserving the pan drippings.

Stir the flour into the reserved pan drippings. Cook until bubbly, stirring constantly. Add the stock, sherry and tarragon and mix well. Cook until thickened, stirring constantly. Stir in the bacon mixture. Spoon the sauce over the quail. Bake, covered, at 350 degrees for 1 hour or until tender. You may substitute dove or chicken for the quail, decreasing the baking time to 30 minutes. A preheated oven is recommended.

99

When James K. Polk died, Sarah Polk determined to manage her late husband's business affairs. The largest of these was a cotton plantation in Mississippi. Nearly one thousand acres were farmed by up to forty slaves. Day-to-day operations were managed by an overseer. Mrs. Polk kept current with plantation affairs through frequent letter-writing to the overseer. She kept close track of cotton production and made sure enough food, shelter, and clothing were provided for her slaves. Her careful management contributed to a successful operation. She managed to turn a profit through the 1850s and sold the plantation very fortuitously in 1860, just prior to the start of the Civil War.

The gardens of the Polk Home are accentuated with English boxwoods and white azaleas. Early 19th-century statues representing the four seasons are located throughout the garden, and an original Polk fountain, dating to the 1820s, is the centerpiece of the courtyard garden.

Seafood Choices

CRUNCHY BAKED CATFISH WITH CREOLE SAUCE
SERVES 4

CREOLE SAUCE

1/2 cup chopped tomato
1/4 cup chopped onion
1/4 cup chopped celery
1/4 cup chopped green bell pepper
2 garlic cloves, chopped
2 teaspoons olive oil
1 teaspoon Greek seasoning
1/4 teaspoon thyme

1/4 teaspoon basil
1/4 teaspoon paprika
1/8 teaspoon red pepper
1/8 teaspoon white pepper
1/8 teaspoon black pepper
3/4 cup chicken broth
1 tablespoon tomato paste

CATFISH

2 eggs
2 tablespoons water
1 cup cracker crumbs
2 tablespoons butter, melted

1 ounce Parmesan cheese, grated
1 tablespoon Greek seasoning
4 catfish fillets
2 tablespoons butter, melted

For the sauce, sauté the tomato, onion, celery, bell pepper and garlic in the olive oil in a skillet over medium-high heat. Stir in the Greek seasoning, thyme, basil, paprika, red pepper, white pepper and black pepper. Add the broth and tomato paste and mix well. Cook for 2 minutes, stirring frequently. Cover to keep warm.

For the fish, whisk the eggs and water in a bowl until blended. Mix the cracker crumbs, 2 tablespoons butter, cheese and Greek seasoning in a shallow dish. Dip each fillet in the egg mixture and coat with the crumb mixture.

Arrange the fillets in a single layer in a buttered 9×13-inch baking dish. Drizzle with 2 tablespoons melted butter. Bake at 350 degrees for 30 minutes. Serve with the sauce. A preheated oven is recommended.

HALIBUT SAUTÉ WITH CAPERS AND MEUNIÈRE SAUCE

S E R V E S 4

30 butter crackers, crushed
3/4 cup (3 ounces) grated Parmesan cheese
4 (8-ounce) halibut fillets, skinned and
cut into pieces
3/4 cup flour
1 cup buttermilk
1/4 cup (1/2 stick) butter
3 tablespoons olive oil
1/4 cup dry white wine
1 to 2 tablespoons drained capers
juice of 1/2 lemon
lemon wedges
sprigs of fresh parsley

Mix the cracker crumbs and cheese in a shallow dish. Coat the fish with the flour and dip in the buttermilk. Roll the fish in the crumb mixture and pat lightly. Arrange the fish on a plate. Chill, covered with waxed paper, for 2 hours.

Heat the butter and olive oil in a large skillet until bubbly. Sauté the fish in the hot butter mixture until the fish flakes easily and is golden brown on both sides. Remove the fish to a platter. Keep warm.

Deglaze the skillet with the wine. Stir in the capers and lemon juice. Simmer just until heated through, stirring constantly. Drizzle the sauce over and around the fish. Garnish with lemon wedges and sprigs of parsley. Serve with your favorite pasta. For thicker pieces, you may finish the cooking process in a 300-degree oven.

ORANGE ROUGHY WITH CUCUMBER AND DILL

S E R V E S 2

1/2 cup mayonnaise
1/2 cup chopped cucumber
2 green onions, chopped
1 tablespoon drained capers (optional)
1 tablespoon chopped fresh dill weed, or
1 teaspoon dried dill weed
1/8 to 1/4 teaspoon hot pepper sauce
salt to taste
2 orange roughy fillets or any firm white
fish fillets
fresh lemon juice
lemon slices

Combine the mayonnaise, cucumber, green onions, capers, dill weed, hot pepper sauce and salt in a bowl and mix well. Arrange the fillets skin side down in a single layer in a baking dish sprayed with nonstick cooking spray. Brush with lemon juice and spread with the mayonnaise mixture. Broil 3 to 5 inches from the heat source for 7 to 10 minutes or until the fillets flake easily and are light brown. Garnish with lemon slices. Serve immediately. A preheated oven is recommended.

MAPLE-GLAZED SALMON

S E R V E S 6

6 tablespoons maple syrup
1/2 cup water
2 garlic cloves, minced
1/2 teaspoon ground ginger, or
1 1/2 tablespoons minced fresh gingerroot
1/2 teaspoon red pepper flakes
1/4 teaspoon salt
6 (6-ounce) salmon fillets

Combine the maple syrup, water, garlic, ginger, red pepper flakes and salt in a saucepan and mix well. Simmer until the mixture is reduced to 1/2 cup, stirring occasionally. Let stand until cool. You may prepare in advance and store, covered, in the refrigerator. Reheat before using.

Arrange the fillets in a single layer on an oiled rack in a broiler pan. Broil 4 inches from the heat source for 5 to 7 minutes. Baste heavily with the maple syrup mixture. Broil for 6 to 8 minutes longer or until the fillets flake easily. A preheated oven is recommended.

BILLY'S SIMPLE SALMON

S E R V E S 2

2 (6-ounce) salmon fillets
1 tablespoon fresh lemon juice
1/2 teaspoon chopped fresh dill weed
mayonnaise to taste

Arrange the fillets skin side up on a microwave-safe plate and cover with plastic wrap. Microwave on Medium for 5 minutes. Turn the fillets and cover with plastic wrap. Microwave on Medium for 5 minutes longer. Drizzle the fillets with the lemon juice and sprinkle with the dill weed. Top each with a dollop of mayonnaise. Serve immediately. You may also serve the salmon with the Artichoke Mayonnaise on page 134 and Cucumber and Dill Sauce on page 135.

Javanese-Roasted Salmon on Wilted Spinach

S E R V E S   8

Soy Lime Sauce

1/2 cup (1 stick) butter
1 teaspoon crushed red pepper
1 large garlic clove, minced
1/2 cup packed light brown sugar

1/2 cup fresh lime juice
1/2 cup soy sauce
2 teaspoons cornstarch
2 teaspoons water

Salmon

3 tablespoons butter
8 (7-ounce) salmon fillets

12 ounces baby spinach, trimmed
salt and pepper to taste

For the sauce, heat the butter in a large heavy saucepan over medium heat. Add the red pepper and garlic and mix well. Cook for 1 minute or until fragrant, stirring constantly. Whisk in the brown sugar until blended. Cook for 4 minutes or until the mixture begins to bubble, whisking frequently. Whisk in the lime juice and soy sauce. Increase the heat to high. Bring to a boil.

Boil for 2 minutes or until the mixture is reduced to 1 1/2 cups, stirring frequently. Dissolve the cornstarch in the water in a small bowl. Add the cornstarch mixture to the lime juice mixture and mix well. Boil for 3 minutes or until thickened, stirring frequently. Remove from the heat. Cover to keep warm.

For the salmon, heat 1 tablespoon of the butter in a skillet over high heat. Sear the fillets in the hot butter for 2 minutes per side or until golden brown. Remove the fillets to a baking sheet. Spoon 1 tablespoon of the sauce over each fillet. Roast at 400 degrees for 5 minutes or until the fillets are opaque in the center.

Heat the remaining 2 tablespoons butter in a large saucepan over medium-high heat. Add the spinach and toss to coat. Cook for 3 minutes or until wilted but bright green, stirring frequently. Season with salt and pepper. Divide the spinach evenly among 8 serving plates. Top each serving with a fillet and drizzle with some of the remaining sauce. Serve immediately. A preheated oven is recommended.

BAKED RED SNAPPER WITH SHRIMP SAUCE

SERVES 8

RED SNAPPER

1 (3-pound) red snapper, cleaned
salt and pepper to taste
butter

Worcestershire sauce to taste
lemon juice to taste

SHRIMP SAUCE

2 tablespoons butter
2 tablespoons flour
1/2 teaspoon salt
2 cups milk
2 hard-cooked eggs, chopped

1 cup deveined peeled cooked shrimp,
chopped
1 (6-ounce) can mushroom
stems and pieces

For the red snapper, rub the inside of the fish with salt, pepper and butter. Rub the outside of the fish with a mixture of Worcestershire sauce and lemon juice. Wrap loosely in foil and arrange on a baking sheet. Bake at 350 degrees for 45 minutes; open the foil. Continue baking until light brown.

For the sauce, heat the butter in a saucepan. Stir in the flour and salt. Cook until bubbly, stirring constantly. Add the milk gradually, cooking and stirring constantly until thickened. Remove from the heat. Stir in the eggs, shrimp and undrained mushrooms. Arrange the red snapper on a heated serving platter. Drizzle with the sauce. Serve immediately. A preheated oven is recommended.

SEARED TUNA WITH WASABI AND PICKLED GINGER

SERVES 4

DRESSING
1/2 cup ponzu or lite soy sauce
1 tablespoon finely chopped fresh gingerroot
1 tablespoon toasted sesame oil

TUNA
4 (6- to 8-ounce) yellowfin or ahi tuna steaks
1/4 cup sesame oil
1 cup black sesame seeds
fresh spinach leaves or arugula
2 teaspoons wasabi paste
1/4 cup pickled ginger

For the dressing, mix the ponzu, gingerroot and sesame oil in a bowl.

For the tuna, rinse each tuna steak and pat dry. Brush the steaks with the sesame oil and coat 1 side of each steak with black sesame seeds. Sear the tuna in a hot skillet for 3 to 4 minutes per side for rare, or 5 to 6 minutes per side for medium-rare. Slice each steak diagonally into strips. Drizzle with the dressing.

Arrange each sliced tuna steak over spinach or arugula on a serving plate. Arrange 1/2 teaspoon of the wasabi paste and 1 tablespoon of the pickled ginger on the side of each serving.

During Sarah Polk's forty-two-year widowhood, she tried determinedly to preserve her husband's legacy. Visitors to her Nashville home, Polk Place, observed that the house was furnished as a museum honoring President Polk. Sarah prominently displayed mementos from Washington, including White House china, the 1846 Presidential portrait by G. P. A. Healy, and framed copies of James K. Polk's Inaugural Address and first Message to Congress. Asked if she ever tired of answering questions about her husband, Sarah replied, "Nothing delighted me more than to resurrect these long-ago facts."

PECAN-CRUSTED TROUT

S E R V E S   4

1 egg
1 tablespoon water
1/4 cup flour
salt and pepper to taste
1/2 cup finely chopped pecans
4 rainbow trout fillets
2 tablespoons olive oil
2 tablespoons butter
chopped fresh parsley
lemon wedges

Whisk the egg and water in a bowl. Mix the flour, salt and pepper in a shallow dish. Stir in the pecans. Dip the fillets in the egg wash and coat with the flour mixture. Heat the olive oil and butter in a large skillet until very hot but not smoking.

Arrange 2 of the fillets flesh side down in the hot oil mixture. Fry until brown on both sides, turning once. Remove the fillets to a heated platter. Repeat the process with the remaining fillets.

Sprinkle 4 heated serving plates with parsley and arrange 1 fillet on each plate. Sprinkle the fillets with additional parsley and garnish with lemon wedges.

VIRGINIA'S CRUSTLESS CRAB PIE

S E R V E S   6

1 1/2 cups milk
4 eggs
1/2 cup chopped green onions
1/3 cup flour
2 tablespoons butter
1 teaspoon salt
1/8 teaspoon (scant) red pepper
1 to 2 tablespoons sherry (optional)
2 cups (8 ounces) shredded Swiss cheese
1 (6-ounce) can lump crab meat, drained
12 fresh asparagus spears, steamed

Process the milk, eggs, green onions, flour, butter, salt, red pepper and sherry in a blender until smooth. Layer the cheese and crab meat in the order listed in a buttered 10-inch round baking dish. Pour the milk mixture over the prepared layers.

Pat the asparagus dry with paper towels. Arrange the spears in a spoke fashion over the top. Bake at 350 degrees for 25 minutes or until puffy and golden brown. Let stand for 10 minutes before serving. A preheated oven is recommended.

CELEBRATION CRAB MEAT AND RICE BAKE

S E R V E S   8

1/4 cup (1/2 stick) butter
1/4 cup flour
2 cups half-and-half
1 tablespoon lemon juice
1 teaspoon salt
1/8 teaspoon red pepper
1/8 teaspoon nutmeg
1 pound fresh crab meat, shells removed and flaked,
or 2 (6-ounce) cans crab meat, drained
2 cups cooked rice
6 tablespoons sherry
buttered cracker crumbs

*H*eat the butter in a saucepan over low heat. Add the flour and mix well. Cook for 3 to 5 minutes or until bubbly, stirring constantly. Stir in the half-and-half gradually. Cook until thickened, stirring constantly. Stir in the lemon juice, salt, red pepper and nutmeg. Add the crab meat, rice and sherry to the cream sauce and mix well.

Spoon the crab meat mixture into a buttered shallow 3-quart baking dish. Sprinkle with cracker crumbs. Bake at 350 degrees for 25 minutes or until brown and bubbly. Serve with a gelatin salad, steamed asparagus, hot rolls and a light dessert at your next luncheon. A preheated oven is recommended.

*S*arah Polk's political interests and involvement displeased traditionalists who expected the First Lady to be primarily a homemaker. Sarah was amused to learn that a fellow townswoman from Columbia, Tennessee, was supporting Henry Clay against James K. Polk in the 1844 Presidential election because of Mrs. Clay's reputation as an accomplished housewife who made excellent butter. Sarah responded, "If I should be so fortunate as to reach the White House, I expect to live on twenty-five thousand dollars a year, and I will neither keep house nor make butter." President Polk's surviving 1846 grocery account book lists "table butter" as a regular purchase.

BAKED OYSTERS ITALIA
S E R V E S   2   T O   4

2 tablespoons butter
1 cup fresh white bread crumbs
1 teaspoon chopped garlic
3 tablespoons chopped fresh flat-leaf parsley
2 dozen fresh oysters, drained
(about two 8-ounce containers)
1/4 cup grated Parmesan cheese
2 tablespoons butter, melted

*H*eat 2 tablespoons butter in a skillet over medium-high heat. Sauté the bread crumbs and garlic in the hot butter for 4 to 5 minutes or until crisp and golden brown. Stir in the parsley. Remove from the heat.

Spread 2/3 of the crumb mixture over the bottom of a buttered 10-inch round baking dish or a dish just large enough to hold the oysters in a single layer. Pat the oysters dry with paper towels and arrange in a single layer over the crumb mixture. Mix the remaining crumb mixture with the cheese and sprinkle over the oysters. Drizzle with 2 tablespoons melted butter. Bake in the top third of the oven at 450 degrees for 12 to 15 minutes or until golden brown and bubbly. Serve immediately. A preheated oven is recommended.

KIERAN'S SCALLOPED OYSTERS
S E R V E S   6   T O   8

1/4 cup chopped celery hearts and leaves
1/4 cup minced green onions
1/2 cup (1 stick) butter
2 pints select raw oysters, drained
salt and pepper to taste
freshly ground nutmeg to taste
saltine cracker crumbs
1 cup half-and-half
shredded Swiss cheese or sharp
Cheddar cheese

*S*auté the celery and green onions in the butter in a skillet until tender. Layer the oysters, green onion mixture, salt, pepper, nutmeg and cracker crumbs 1/2 at a time in a buttered 2-quart baking dish. Insert a knife blade in several places around the edge of the baking dish and in the center of the oyster mixture, pouring the half-and-half around the blade. Bake, covered, at 400 degrees for 30 minutes. Remove the cover and sprinkle with cheese. Bake for 10 minutes longer. A preheated oven is recommended.

SEA SCALLOPS WITH COUSCOUS

SERVES 4

1 pound sea scallops
freshly ground pepper
3 tablespoons olive oil
1/4 cup sherry
2 1/2 cups chicken stock
3 tablespoons butter
1 tablespoon chopped fresh thyme
1/8 teaspoon saffron
2 cups couscous

Remove the muscle from each scallop and discard. Sprinkle with pepper. Sauté the scallops in the olive oil in a skillet for 1 minute or until golden brown and caramelized. Remove the scallops to a platter using a slotted spoon. Cover to keep warm.

Drain any remaining oil from the skillet. Deglaze the skillet with the sherry, stirring with a wooden spoon to release any browned bits from the side and bottom of the skillet. Simmer until the sherry is reduced by 2/3, stirring occasionally. Stir in the stock, butter, thyme and saffron.

Bring to a boil and stir in the couscous. Remove from the heat and cover. Let stand for 5 minutes and fluff with a fork. Serve the couscous with the scallops.

Sarah Polk lived longer as a widow than any other First Lady. Three months after leaving the White House, James K. Polk died of cholera in June 1849. Sarah was only forty-five years old at the time. She stayed in Nashville at Polk Place, the President's intended retirement home, until her death in August 1891. She never remarried and wore black all forty-two years of her widowhood. When she died, she was buried with her husband on the grounds of Polk Place. Their tomb was moved to the Tennessee State Capitol in 1893.

FESTIVE FETTUCCINI WITH SCALLOPS AND RED PEPPER CREAM SAUCE

SERVES 6

RED PEPPER CREAM SAUCE

3 large red bell peppers
1/2 cup pine nuts or chopped
   pecans, toasted
1/2 cup (2 ounces) grated
   Parmesan cheese

1/4 cup olive oil
1 tablespoon minced garlic
1 cup whipping cream
salt and pepper to taste

SCALLOPS

6 tablespoons olive oil
1/4 cup dry white wine
3 tablespoons minced garlic
1 1/2 teaspoons oregano
1/2 teaspoon seasoned salt

1/2 teaspoon paprika
1/2 teaspoon chili powder
1 1/2 pounds sea scallops
1 pound spinach fettuccini
chopped fresh parsley to taste

For the sauce, arrange the bell peppers on a baking sheet. Broil until blackened, turning frequently. Place the bell peppers in a sealable plastic bag and seal tightly. Let stand for 10 minutes. Peel, seed and coarsely chop the bell peppers. Process the bell peppers, pine nuts, cheese, olive oil and garlic in a food processor until the bell peppers are finely chopped. Combine the bell pepper mixture, whipping cream, salt and pepper in a bowl and mix well. Chill, covered, in the refrigerator.

For the scallops, whisk the olive oil, wine, garlic, oregano, seasoned salt, paprika and chili powder in a bowl. Add the scallops and toss to coat. Marinate, covered, in the refrigerator for 3 to 10 hours, stirring occasionally.

Cook the pasta using package directions until al dente; drain. Cover to keep warm. Heat a heavy skillet over medium heat. Remove the scallops from the marinade; do not totally drain. Sauté the scallops in the hot skillet for 1 minute per side or until opaque. Reheat the sauce in a saucepan over low heat, stirring occasionally. Combine the pasta with the desired amount of the sauce in a pasta bowl and mix well. Top with the scallops and sprinkle with parsley. Serve immediately.

SHRIMP CAPTIVA
S E R V E S 4

3 garlic cloves, minced
2 tablespoons olive oil
1 (14-ounce) can diced tomatoes
1 (14-ounce) can artichoke hearts, drained
and cut into quarters
2 tablespoons pesto
1 tablespoon drained capers
1 tablespoon fresh lemon juice
1 pound shrimp, peeled and deveined
4 ounces feta cheese, crumbled
salt and freshly ground pepper to taste
8 ounces spaghetti, cooked and drained

*S*auté the garlic in the olive oil in a large skillet. Stir in the undrained tomatoes, artichokes, pesto, capers and lemon juice. Cook for 3 minutes or until the liquid is slightly reduced, stirring frequently. Stir in the shrimp.

Cook for 2 minutes or until the shrimp turn pink, stirring frequently. Add the cheese and mix well. Cook until the cheese begins to melt, stirring frequently. Season with salt and pepper. Spoon over hot cooked spaghetti on a serving platter.

SHRIMP AND YELLOW GRITS
S E R V E S 4

3 cups chicken broth
1 cup yellow grits
1/2 cup whipping cream
salt and white pepper to taste
2 tablespoons chopped onion
2 tablespoons chopped green bell pepper
3 tablespoons bacon drippings
1 1/2 cups deveined peeled shrimp
1 1/2 tablespoons flour
1 cup (or more) water
1 tablespoon Worcestershire sauce
1 tablespoon ketchup
salt and pepper to taste

*B*ring the broth to a boil in a saucepan. Whisk in the grits. Cook for 4 minutes or until thickened, whisking frequently. Remove from the heat. Stir in the whipping cream. Season with salt and white pepper. Cover to keep warm.

Sauté the onion and bell pepper in the bacon drippings in a skillet until golden brown. Stir in the shrimp. Cook for 5 minutes or until the shrimp turn pink, stirring frequently. Add the flour and stir until mixed. Stir in the water, Worcestershire sauce, ketchup, salt and pepper. Cook over low heat until thickened, stirring constantly. Spoon over the grits on serving plates.

SHRIMP CHEESECAKE WITH CREOLE MUSTARD

S E R V E S   8

CRUST

*1 cup (4 ounces) grated
Parmesan cheese*

*1 cup bread crumbs
1/2 cup (1 stick) butter, melted*

SHRIMP CHEESECAKE

*1 cup chopped onion
1/2 cup chopped carrots
1/2 cup chopped bell pepper
1 tablespoon olive oil
salt and pepper to taste
24 ounces cream cheese, softened*

*4 eggs
1 cup (4 ounces) shredded smoked
Gouda cheese
1/2 cup heavy cream
1 pound shrimp, cooked, peeled,
deveined and finely chopped*

CREOLE MUSTARD

*3 tablespoons Creole mustard or
whole grain mustard
2 tablespoons (heaping) mayonnaise
1 cup olive oil
2 tablespoons chopped fresh parsley*

*1 tablespoon honey
1 tablespoon white vinegar
1/2 teaspoon salt
1/8 teaspoon cayenne pepper*

For the crust, combine the cheese, bread crumbs and butter in a bowl and mix well. Press the crumb mixture over the bottom of a greased 9-inch springform pan.

For the cheesecake, sauté the onion, carrots and bell pepper in the olive oil in a skillet for 3 to 4 minutes. Season with salt and pepper. Beat the cream cheese and eggs in a mixing bowl until light and fluffy, scraping the bowl occasionally. Add the sautéed vegetables, Gouda cheese, heavy cream and shrimp to the cream cheese mixture and beat until mixed.

Spoon the shrimp mixture into the prepared pan. Bake at 350 degrees for 1 1/4 hours or until a knife inserted in the center comes out clean. Cool slightly in pan on a wire rack.

For the mustard, process the Creole mustard and mayonnaise in a food processor or blender until blended. Add the olive oil gradually, processing constantly until thickened. Add the parsley, honey, vinegar, salt and cayenne pepper. Pulse to blend. Chill, covered, for 30 minutes. Serve the cheesecake hot or warm topped with the desired amount of the mustard. The quality of the mustard is best when served within 24 hours. A preheated oven is recommended.

SEAFOOD AND ARTICHOKE MEDLEY

S E R V E S   1 0   T O   1 2

1¹/2 pounds mushrooms, sliced
2 tablespoons butter
1¹/2 pounds deveined peeled cooked shrimp or crab
meat or a combination of the two
1¹/2 cups chopped cooked chicken breasts, or
1 pound pulled smoked chicken
2 (14-ounce) cans artichoke hearts,
drained and coarsely chopped
³/4 cup (1¹/2 sticks) butter
³/4 cup flour
3 cups milk
¹/2 cup sherry
1 tablespoon Worcestershire sauce
¹/4 teaspoon paprika
salt and pepper to taste
¹/2 to 1 cup (2 to 4 ounces) freshly grated
Parmesan cheese

Sauté the mushrooms in 2 tablespoons butter in a skillet until tender. Layer the mushrooms, shrimp, chicken and artichokes in a greased shallow 3-quart baking dish.

Heat ³/4 cup butter in a saucepan over low heat. Add the flour and mix well. Cook until bubbly, stirring constantly. Add the milk gradually, whisking constantly. Cook until thickened, whisking constantly. Stir in the sherry, Worcestershire sauce, paprika, salt and pepper. Spoon the sauce over the prepared layers and sprinkle with the cheese. Bake at 350 degrees for 40 minutes or until brown and bubbly. A preheated oven is recommended.

A couple of months before her eighty-fifth birthday, Sarah Polk officially opened the 1888 Cincinnati Centennial Exposition without leaving her Nashville home. To afford her this honor, Western Union connected telegraph wire to Polk Place. Surrounded by local dignitaries, Sarah pushed an electric button and soon received this dispatch from Cincinnati: "When Mrs. Polk touched the key, the machinery started, bells rang, hundreds of electric lights flashed out, and the entire concourse of people rose and cheered amid the waving of flags and banners. Such a thrilling scene has not been witnessed for years."

15. Received Cash of Mrs. Smith   30 " .

16. 14 Chickens   2 " .   20 Bought

"   1 Leg of Veal   " 96.   " 62½ Bushel

"   12 ℔ of Pork   " 96   "   Paid for

"   9 ℔ of Beef   " 72   "   Paid the

"   2 Quarters of Mutton   1 50.

"   4 Quarts of Rasp berries   " 80   15 from to Roll

18 13½ ℔ of Butter for the Hals   2. 70.

"   3 Doz of Eggs   " 48   Received pay in full

"   1 peck Potatoes   37.   H. Bowman B

"   1 Leg of Mutton   " 60   June 22. Received Cash

"   1 Rack of Mutton   37   "   " 1 Bushel

"   9 ℔ of Beef   " 72   " 23 3 Bills

20 ..   fish for the Servants   " 25   "   20 ℔ Bu

"   5 ℔ of Table Butter No Q   1 56   "   10½ ℔

"   Soup Meat —   " 50   "   12 ℔

"   21½ ℔ of Mutton   1 37   "   25 ℔

"   12 ℔ of Veal   " 96   "   1 Sh

"   2 Doz of Eggs   32.   "   3 Doz

"   Paid for Yeast   " 25   "   1 ℔

                        Total   14 . 39.   25   1 fine

                                                              "   13½ ℔

This grocery account book was kept by White House steward Henry Bowman, a man James K. Polk called "the most faithful man I have ever known." Bowman carefully recorded the amount and cost of food and wine being supplied to the Polk White House. It is astonishing proof of the lavish scale of dining that took place during the Polk administration.

ASPARAGUS TARRAGON
S E R V E S   4   T O   6

1 pound asparagus spears
2 tablespoons olive oil
1 tablespoon chopped fresh tarragon, or
1 teaspoon dried tarragon
1/4 teaspoon salt

Snap off the woody ends of the asparagus spears. Arrange the spears in a shallow dish. Whisk the olive oil, tarragon and salt in a bowl. Pour the olive oil mixture over the asparagus and turn to coat.

Arrange the asparagus in a single layer on a grill rack or in a grill basket. Grill over medium heat for 3 minutes; turn. Grill for 4 minutes longer or to the desired degree of crispness. Or, arrange the asparagus in a single layer in a baking dish. Broil 4 inches from the heat source for 5 minutes, turning once.

BROCCOLI WITH HORSERADISH SAUCE
S E R V E S   6   T O   8

HORSERADISH SAUCE

3/4 cup mayonnaise
1 or 2 hard-cooked eggs, chopped (optional)
1/4 cup (1/2 stick) butter, melted
1 tablespoon horseradish
1 tablespoon grated onion
1/4 teaspoon salt
1/4 teaspoon dry mustard
1/8 teaspoon red pepper

BROCCOLI

1 bunch broccoli, trimmed and
cut into spears
salt to taste

For the sauce, combine the mayonnaise, eggs, butter, horseradish, onion, salt, dry mustard and red pepper in a bowl and mix well.

For the broccoli, combine the broccoli and salt with enough water to cover in a saucepan. Bring to a boil. Boil for 8 minutes or to the desired degree of crispness; drain. Spoon the sauce over the warm broccoli in a serving bowl. You may steam the broccoli if preferred.

VERMICELLI AND BROCCOLI

SERVES 6

1/4 cup (1/2 stick) butter
2 tablespoons chopped onion
1 (10-ounce) package frozen broccoli florets, or florets
of 2 bunches broccoli
1/2 cup sliced mushrooms
3 cups half-and-half
3/4 cup (1 1/2 sticks) butter, sliced
1/4 teaspoon nutmeg
salt and pepper to taste
6 egg yolks, beaten
16 ounces vermicelli, cooked and drained
. 1/2 cup (2 ounces) grated Parmesan cheese
chopped fresh parsley

Heat 1/4 cup butter in a medium saucepan. Cook the onion in the butter until tender, stirring constantly. Stir in the broccoli and mushrooms. Cook for 2 minutes, stirring frequently. Stir in the half-and-half, 3/4 cup butter, nutmeg, salt and pepper.

Bring just to a boil, stirring occasionally. Stir a small amount of the hot mixture into the egg yolks. Stir the egg yolks into the hot mixture. Simmer just until heated through, stirring frequently. Add the pasta and toss to coat. Stir in the cheese. Spoon the broccoli mixture onto heated serving plates or a heated serving platter. Sprinkle with parsley. Add 1 cup chopped cooked chicken for a one-dish meal.

Two weeks before leaving the Presidency, James K. Polk startled his wife by revealing that he had written and signed his Last Will and Testament that afternoon. His preparations were fortuitous. When he died unexpectedly less than four months later, Sarah received an ample inheritance of land, money, and personal property. By prudently managing these resources, she maintained a home in Nashville and lived comfortably, unlike many other widowed First Ladies who experienced financial hardship. The federal government did not provide a regular pension for Presidential widows until the 1880s following James A. Garfield's assassination.

CARROT SOUFFLÉ
SERVES 8

2 cups (2 pounds) mashed cooked carrots
1 cup cracker crumbs
1 cup milk
3/4 cup (3 ounces) shredded sharp
Cheddar cheese
1/2 cup (1 stick) butter, softened
1/4 cup grated onion
1 teaspoon salt
1/4 teaspoon black pepper
1/8 teaspoon cayenne pepper
3 eggs, beaten
1/4 to 1/3 cup shredded sharp
Cheddar cheese

Combine the carrots, cracker crumbs, milk,
3/4 cup cheese, butter, onion, salt, black pepper
and cayenne pepper in a bowl and mix gently.
Fold in the eggs. Spoon the carrot mixture into
a deep baking dish or 10-inch soufflé dish.
Sprinkle with 1/4 to 1/3 cup cheese. Bake at
350 degrees for 40 to 45 minutes or until light
brown and puffy. A preheated oven is
recommended.

SOUTHERN FRIED CORN
SERVES 8

8 ears of fresh corn, shucked and
silks removed
3 tablespoons unsalted butter, melted
1 teaspoon each salt and sugar
1/4 teaspoon pepper

Cut the tops of the corn kernels with a sharp
knife into a saucepan. Using the back of a knife,
scrape the cobs to release the milk into the
saucepan. Stir in the remaining ingredients.
Cook for 8 to 10 minutes, stirring occasionally.

CORN PUDDING
SERVES 12

3 (10-ounce) packages frozen
white corn, thawed
3 1/2 pints whipping cream
8 eggs, lightly beaten
1/4 cup sugar
1 tablespoon salt
1/8 teaspoon red pepper

Process the corn in a food processor until
blended. Combine with the remaining ingredients
in a bowl and mix well. Spoon the corn mixture
into a 3-quart baking dish sprayed with nonstick
cooking spray. Bake at 325 degrees for 1 1/4 hours
or until a knife inserted in the center comes out
clean. A preheated oven is recommended.

GREEN BEANS WITH HONEY-ROASTED PECANS

S E R V E S   6

HONEY-ROASTED PECANS
3/4 cup pecan halves
1 tablespoon honey

GREEN BEANS
1¼ pounds fresh green beans, trimmed
½ cup chicken stock
1 teaspoon peanut oil
¼ cup julienned red bell pepper

For the pecans, toss the pecans with the honey in a bowl. Spread the honey-coated pecans in a single layer on an oiled baking sheet. Roast at 400 degrees for 8 minutes, stirring occasionally. Remove the pecans to a sheet of waxed paper or foil to cool.

For the beans, combine the beans, stock and peanut oil in a saucepan. Cook, covered, over high heat for 3 minutes; remove the cover. Cook over medium heat until the stock evaporates and the beans are tender-crisp, stirring occasionally. Spoon the beans into a serving bowl. Top with the pecans and bell pepper strips. A preheated oven is recommended.

Early in her widowhood, Sarah Polk received the sad news that her niece Mary Jetton had died, leaving behind a young daughter. Although Sarah had never been a mother, she agreed to raise the girl. A friend expressed surprise: "You are not the one, Madame, to have the charge of a little child; you, who have always been absorbed in political and social affairs." Sallie Jetton grew up at Sarah's home in Nashville and provided constant companionship for the former First Lady. When Sallie married local merchant George William Fall, Sarah persuaded the couple to stay with her at Polk Place.

GREEN BEANS WITH OVEN-ROASTED ONION SLIVERS

S E R V E S 8

*2 pounds fresh small green beans,
trimmed
country bacon
3 medium onions
2 tablespoons butter, melted*

*salt and pepper to taste
1 cup chicken stock
1 1/2 tablespoons sugar
1 tablespoon red wine vinegar*

Combine the beans and desired amount of bacon with enough water to cover in a saucepan. Bring to a boil; reduce the heat. Simmer just until the beans are tender; drain. Cover to keep warm. Line a large heavy baking sheet with heavy-duty foil and spray the foil with nonstick cooking spray.

Slice each onion into 12 to 14 wedges. Cut off the root ends to form onion slivers. Spread the onion slivers in a single layer on the prepared baking sheet and drizzle with the melted butter. Sprinkle with salt and pepper. Roast at 450 degrees for 30 to 35 minutes or until the onions are dark brown on the underside.

Pour the stock into a heavy saucepan or skillet. Bring to a boil over high heat. Boil for 5 to 6 minutes or until the broth is reduced to 1/4 cup. Stir in the sugar and vinegar. Bring to a boil. Boil until the sugar dissolves, stirring frequently. Stir in the onions. Reduce the heat to medium-low.

Simmer for 5 minutes or until the liquid is slightly reduced, stirring occasionally. Season with salt and pepper. Pour the hot sauce over the hot beans in a serving bowl. The sauce may be prepared a day in advance, stored in the refrigerator and reheated before serving. A preheated oven is recommended.

PORTOBELLO MUSHROOM BURGERS

S E R V E S 4

1/4 cup balsamic vinegar
2 tablespoons olive oil
1/4 cup chopped fresh basil
1 garlic clove, minced
1/4 teaspoon salt
1/4 teaspoon freshly ground pepper
1 red bell pepper, cut into 8 strips
1 yellow bell pepper, cut into 8 strips
1 sweet onion, cut into 8 slices
8 portobello mushroom caps
4 (1-ounce) slices part-skim mozzarella cheese

Mix the vinegar, olive oil, basil, garlic, salt and pepper in a shallow dish or large sealable plastic bag. Add the bell peppers and onion to the vinegar mixture and mix well. Marinate, covered, in the refrigerator for 30 minutes, stirring occasionally. Add the mushroom caps to the bell pepper mixture and turn to coat. Marinate, covered, in the refrigerator for 30 minutes longer. Drain, reserving the marinade.

Arrange the bell pepper strips on a grill rack. Grill, with the lid down, over medium-high heat (350 to 400 degrees) for 10 minutes or until partially charred. Arrange 4 mushroom caps upside down on the grill rack and top evenly with the grilled bell peppers and cheese. Top with the remaining mushroom caps right side up to form a burger.

Grill, with the lid down, over medium-high heat until the cheese melts, turning once. Serve with the reserved marinade. You may slice each burger and serve over hot cooked rice. Sauté or broil the vegetables instead of grilling if desired.

Forty years after James K. Polk's victory in the 1844 Presidential election, his eighty-one-year-old widow was interviewed for a Nashville newspaper article. When the journalist asked Mrs. Polk to reminisce about the election, she modestly responded, "So many years have elapsed since that event that the facts have almost faded from my memory." Then she quickly disproved her statement by giving knowledgeable explanations of 1844 campaign issues such as westward expansion and the reduction of tariffs. She proudly described the Polk Administration's acquisition of the Southwest from Texas to California as "among the most important events in the history of this country."

MUSHROOMS AU GRATIN

S E R V E S   4

1 pound mushrooms, trimmed and sliced
2 tablespoons butter
1/8 teaspoon cayenne pepper
salt and black pepper to taste
1 tablespoon butter
1 tablespoon flour
1 cup milk
1/4 cup heavy cream
3 tablespoons bread crumbs
2 tablespoons grated Parmesan cheese

Sauté the mushrooms in 2 tablespoons butter in a skillet. Spoon the mushrooms into a baking dish. Sprinkle with cayenne pepper, salt and black pepper.

Heat 1 tablespoon butter in a saucepan. Stir in the flour until blended. Add the milk and mix well. Bring to a boil. Boil for 1 minute, stirring frequently. Stir in the heavy cream. Pour the cream mixture over the mushrooms. Sprinkle with the bread crumbs and cheese. Bake at 400 degrees for 10 minutes. A preheated oven is recommended.

POTATOES ANNA

S E R V E S   8

1 teaspoon sea salt or kosher salt
1/2 teaspoon pepper
2 1/2 tablespoons butter
3 pounds baking potatoes, peeled and
cut into 1/8-inch slices
1 tablespoon butter, melted
1 tablespoon chopped fresh parsley

Mix the salt and pepper in a small bowl. Heat 2 1/2 tablespoons butter in a cast-iron skillet or ovenproof skillet over medium heat. Arrange a single layer of potatoes slightly overlapping in a circular pattern in the prepared skillet. Sprinkle with 1/4 of the salt mixture and drizzle with some of the melted butter. Repeat the layering process 5 times with the remaining potatoes, remaining salt mixture and remaining melted butter, ending with melted butter. Press firmly to pack.

Bake, covered, at 450 degrees for 20 minutes; remove the cover. Bake for 25 minutes longer or until golden brown. Run a sharp knife around the edge of the skillet to loosen the potatoes. Place a plate upside down over the top of the skillet and invert the potatoes onto the plate. Sprinkle with the parsley. A preheated oven is recommended.

ROASTED ROSEMARY POTATOES

S E R V E S   1 0

1/4 cup olive oil
2 tablespoons chopped fresh rosemary
1¹/2 teaspoons kosher salt
1 teaspoon freshly ground pepper
4 garlic cloves, chopped
3 pounds small potatoes, cut into
halves or quarters

*M*ix the olive oil, rosemary, salt, pepper and garlic in a shallow dish. Add the potatoes and toss to coat. Arrange the potatoes in a single layer on a baking sheet. Roast at 400 degrees for 1 hour or until crisp, turning once or twice. A preheated oven is recommended.

ANN'S ORANGE-GLAZED SWEET POTATOES

S E R V E S   4   T O   6

2 pounds sweet potatoes, peeled and
sliced lengthwise into halves
²/3 cup sugar
1 tablespoon cornstarch
1 teaspoon salt
1 teaspoon grated orange zest
1 cup orange juice
2 tablespoons butter

*A*rrange the sweet potatoes in a shallow baking dish. Combine the sugar, cornstarch, salt and orange zest in a bowl and mix well. Stir in the orange juice. Heat the butter in a saucepan. Stir the orange juice mixture into the butter.

Cook until thickened, stirring frequently. Continue cooking for 1 minute longer, stirring frequently. Spoon the orange sauce over the sweet potatoes. Bake, covered, at 400 degrees for 1 hour or until the sweet potatoes are tender. A preheated oven is recommended.

SPINACH SOUFFLÉ

S E R V E S   8

*1 (10-ounce) package frozen chopped
spinach, cooked and drained
1/4 cup (1/2 stick) butter
1/4 cup flour
3/4 cup milk
1/2 teaspoon salt
1/8 teaspoon pepper
1 cup (4 ounces) shredded sharp
Cheddar cheese
2 tablespoons chopped onion (optional)
4 egg yolks, lightly beaten
4 egg whites*

Press the excess moisture from the spinach. Heat the butter in a saucepan over low heat. Stir in the flour. Cook until smooth and bubbly, stirring constantly. Add the milk gradually, stirring constantly. Stir in the salt and pepper. Cook over medium heat until thickened, stirring constantly. Stir in the cheese. Cook until blended, stirring constantly. Remove from the heat.

Add the spinach and onion to the cheese sauce and mix well. Add the egg yolks gradually and mix well. Let stand until cool. Beat the egg whites in a mixing bowl until stiff peaks form. Fold the egg whites into the spinach mixture.

Pour the egg mixture into a lightly greased 2-quart soufflé dish or 8 individual soufflé dishes. Bake at 350 degrees for 35 minutes. Serve immediately. For variety, bake the spinach mixture in well-drained fresh tomato cups. A preheated oven is recommended.

CREAMED SPINACH

S E R V E S   4

*1 medium onion, chopped
1 garlic clove, crushed
1/4 cup (1/2 stick) butter
1 pound baby spinach, stems removed, or
regular spinach, torn
1/2 cup sour cream
1/4 teaspoon pepper
1/8 teaspoon salt
1/8 teaspoon nutmeg
paprika to taste*

Sauté the onion and garlic in the butter in a skillet until the onion is tender. Stir in the spinach. Cook until tender, stirring frequently. Stir in the sour cream, pepper, salt and nutmeg.

Cook over low heat until heated through, stirring frequently. Spoon the spinach mixture into a serving bowl and sprinkle with paprika. Serve immediately.

APPLE-STUFFED ACORN SQUASH

SERVES 8

*4 small to medium acorn squash, cut
lengthwise into halves and seeded
3/4 cup packed brown sugar
2 teaspoons lemon juice
1/4 teaspoon ginger
4 Granny Smith apples, peeled and sliced or
chopped into small pieces
salt and pepper to taste
6 tablespoons butter, melted*

Arrange the squash cut side down in a
buttered baking dish. Bake at 350 degrees for
35 minutes or until tender.

Combine the brown sugar, lemon juice and
ginger in a bowl and mix well. Add the apples
and toss to coat.

Turn the squash halves over and sprinkle
with salt and pepper. Stuff some of the apple
mixture into each squash half and drizzle with
melted butter. Bake for 25 minutes. You may
substitute you favorite variety of apples for
the Granny Smith apples. A preheated oven
is recommended.

SQUASH CASSEROLE

SERVES 6

*1 1/2 pounds yellow squash, coarsely chopped
1 medium onion, chopped
salt to taste
3/4 cup (3 ounces) shredded Cheddar cheese
1/4 cup milk or cream
2 tablespoons butter or margarine
1 tablespoon sugar
pepper to taste
1/4 cup (1 ounce) shredded Cheddar cheese
1/2 cup butter cracker crumbs*

Combine the squash, onion and salt with
enough water to cover in a saucepan. Bring to a
boil. Boil until the squash is tender; drain well.
Combine the squash mixture, 3/4 cup cheese,
milk, butter, sugar, salt and pepper in a bowl
and mix well.

Spoon the squash mixture into a 1- to
1 1/2-quart baking dish. Sprinkle with 1/4 cup
cheese and cracker crumbs. Bake at 350 degrees
for 25 minutes or until brown and bubbly. A
preheated oven is recommended.

GREEN TOMATO CASSEROLE

SERVES 6

8 medium green tomatoes, cut into
1/4-inch slices
1 bunch green onions, finely chopped
celery seeds to taste
curry powder to taste
salt and pepper to taste
2 tablespoons chives
2 tablespoons butter
1 cup bread crumbs
3/4 cup (3 ounces) grated Parmesan cheese

Layer the tomatoes and green onions in a baking dish until all the ingredients are used, sprinkling each layer with celery seeds, curry powder, salt, pepper and chives. Dot with the butter and sprinkle with the bread crumbs and cheese. Bake at 350 degrees for 1 hour. This recipe should only be prepared when tomatoes are in season. A preheated oven is recommended.

SLOW-ROASTED TOMATOES

SERVES 8 TO 10

4 pounds small to medium plum, Roma or other firm tomatoes, cut into halves
6 garlic cloves, minced
5 tablespoons olive oil
salt and pepper to taste
minced fresh herbs of choice (optional)

Arrange the tomatoes cut side up in 2 large shallow baking dishes or on 2 baking sheets. Mix the garlic and olive oil in a bowl and drizzle over the tomatoes. Sprinkle with salt, pepper and fresh herbs. Roast at 200 degrees for 6 to 8 hours. Tomatoes will shrink during cooking. Serve hot, warm or at room temperature. You may prepare in advance and store in an airtight container in the refrigerator for up to 1 week. Bring to room temperature before serving. A preheated oven is recommended.

TOMATOES WITH SPINACH CROWNS

S E R V E S   6

1 (10-ounce) package frozen chopped spinach
1/2 cup (2 ounces) grated Parmesan cheese
1/3 cup herb-seasoned stuffing mix, crushed
3 or 4 green onions, minced
3 tablespoons butter, melted
1 egg, beaten
1/2 teaspoon minced garlic
1/4 teaspoon salt
1/4 teaspoon black pepper
6 thick unpeeled tomato slices
garlic salt to taste
cayenne pepper to taste

Cook the spinach using package directions; drain. Press the excess moisture from the spinach. Combine the spinach, cheese, stuffing mix, green onions, butter, egg, minced garlic, salt and black pepper in a bowl and mix well.

Arrange the tomato slices in a single layer in a greased baking dish. Sprinkle with garlic salt. Spoon some of the spinach mixture on top of each tomato slice. Bake at 350 degrees for 15 minutes. Sprinkle with cayenne pepper. You may prepare the spinach topping in advance and store, covered, in the refrigerator. Or, freeze the spinach mixture in individual portions for future use. A preheated oven is recommended.

The first women's rights convention was held in Seneca Falls, New York, in 1848. Although First Lady Sarah Polk made no public statement about the controversial event, her intellectual interests and political activities revealed her disregard for traditional social restrictions. Nearly forty years later, Sarah commented, "It is beautiful to see how women are supporting themselves, and how those who go forward independently in various callings are respected and admired for their energy and industry. It is now considered proper for young ladies, when they leave school, to teach or to do something else for themselves. It was not so in my young days."

CORN BREAD SAGE DRESSING

SERVES 12

3 cups self-rising cornmeal
1/4 cup flour
1 tablespoon sugar
1 teaspoon salt
1/8 teaspoon baking soda
3 cups buttermilk
3 eggs, beaten
1 1/2 cups chopped celery

3/4 cup chopped onion
1 tablespoon bacon drippings
2 cups herb-seasoned stuffing mix
1 (10-ounce) can cream of
    chicken soup
3 to 4 cups chicken broth
3 tablespoons chopped fresh sage
freshly ground pepper to taste

Combine the self-rising cornmeal, flour, sugar, salt and baking soda in a bowl and mix gently. Add the buttermilk and eggs and mix well. Stir in the celery and onion.

Heat the bacon drippings in a 10-inch cast-iron skillet at 450 degrees. Maintain the oven temperature. Stir 1 teaspoon of the hot bacon drippings into the corn bread batter. Spoon the corn bread batter into the hot skillet. Bake at 450 degrees for 30 minutes. Cool slightly and crumble the corn bread into a large bowl. Add the stuffing mix to the corn bread and mix well. Add the soup and broth gradually, stirring constantly to mix. Stir in the sage and pepper.

Spoon the dressing mixture into a greased 9×13-inch baking dish. Bake at 375 degrees for 40 to 45 minutes or until brown and crisp. You may prepare in advance, partially bake, and store, covered, in the freezer. Thaw in the refrigerator before completing the baking process. A preheated oven is recommended.

GARLIC CHEESE GRITS

SERVES 16

8 cups water
2 teaspoons salt
2 cups grits
1 (6-ounce) refrigerator roll garlic cheese, cubed
8 ounces sharp Cheddar cheese, shredded
1/2 cup (1 stick) butter
2 eggs, beaten
1 teaspoon Tabasco sauce
1/4 teaspoon Worcestershire sauce
paprika to taste

*B*ring the water and salt to a boil in a saucepan. Whisk in the grits. Cook until thickened, stirring occasionally. Stir in the garlic cheese, Cheddar cheese, butter, eggs, Tabasco sauce and Worcestershire sauce.

Spoon the grits mixture into a shallow 3-quart baking dish. Sprinkle with paprika. Bake at 350 degrees for 45 minutes. A preheated oven is recommended.

*S*arah Childress, while a student at the Moravian Academy in Salem, North Carolina, enjoyed a wonderfully varied and enlightened education for the period. Students learned such subjects as reading, grammar, writing, arithmetic, history, geography, and plain needlework. If desired (and for a little more tuition), students could also learn music, fine needlework, and drawing. A single example of Sarah's needlework has survived. It is a piece of mourning embroidery of silk and wool stitched into silk, enhanced with watercolors. A beautiful piece that illustrates the high quality of instruction at the school, it is considered one of the finest existing pieces of 19th-century schoolgirl art.

CUMIN RICE PILAF

S E R V E S   1 0   T O   1 2

1 large onion, finely chopped or thinly sliced
6 tablespoons canola oil
6 cups water
8 whole cloves
1 (2-inch) cinnamon stick
1 teaspoon whole cumin seeds
3 cups basmati rice, rinsed and drained
salt to taste

Sauté the onion in the oil in a Dutch oven until light brown. Add the water, cloves, cinnamon stick and cumin seeds. Bring to a boil. Stir in the rice and return the mixture to a boil. Boil, covered, for 1 to 3 minutes. Bake at 325 degrees for 20 minutes, stirring once or twice. Discard the cloves and cinnamon stick. Season with salt. A preheated oven is recommended.

COMPANY RICE

S E R V E S   8

1 cup rice
1/2 cup (1 stick) butter
2 (14-ounce) cans beef consommé
1 cup chopped onion
1/2 cup seedless raisins (optional)
1/2 cup sliced almonds
1 (4-ounce) can sliced mushrooms, drained
1/4 cup dark brown wild rice

Brown 1 cup rice in the butter in a skillet, stirring frequently. Stir in the consommé, onion, raisins, almonds, mushrooms and wild rice. Spoon the rice mixture into a 9×13-inch baking dish. Bake at 350 degrees for 50 to 60 minutes or until the rice is tender. A preheated oven is recommended.

GREEN RICE

S E R V E S   8

3 tablespoons butter
1 cup chopped onion
2 garlic cloves, crushed
2 cups rice
2 (14-ounce) cans chicken broth
1 (14-ounce) can tomatillos, drained and chopped
1 (4-ounce) can chopped green chiles
1/4 cup chopped fresh cilantro

Heat the butter in a large skillet over medium-high heat. Sauté the onion and garlic in the butter for 3 to 5 minutes or until the onion is light brown. Stir in the rice, broth, tomatillos and green chiles. Bring to a boil, stirring occasionally; reduce the heat.

Simmer, covered, over low heat for 20 to 25 minutes or until the liquid is absorbed and the rice is tender. Remove from the heat. Stir in the cilantro.

POLK PICKLES

M A K E S   1   G A L L O N

1/2 package pickling spices
1 gallon sour jumbo pickles, drained
4 1/2 pounds sugar
2 heads garlic, separated into cloves

Wrap the pickling spices in cheesecloth and secure with kitchen twine. Cut the tips from the ends of the pickles and discard. Cut each pickle into 1/4- to 1/2-inch slices. Alternate layers of the sliced pickles, sugar and garlic cloves in a 2-gallon crock until all of the ingredients are used. Add the cheesecloth bag. Let stand, covered, at room temperature for 5 days, stirring each morning. Transfer the pickle mixture to a gallon jar, discarding the spices and garlic. Store, covered, in the refrigerator.

Miss Emma Porter Armstrong, a dedicated Polk Association member, created a legacy for the Spring Polk Pilgrimage Luncheon. For many years, she prepared memorable menus for the celebratory occasion serving both the Nashville and Columbia memberships. She is remembered for the many classic dishes that she prepared, including almond chicken salad, tomato aspic with homemade mayonnaise, squash casserole with sharp Cheddar cheese, country ham biscuits, dessert tart, and the beloved Polk Pickles. Today, the Spring Pilgrimage Luncheon is catered, but the Polk Pickles are still prepared by the membership and served as a tribute to Miss Emma Porter Armstrong and her southern hospitality.

ARTICHOKE MAYONNAISE

VARIABLE

2 (15-ounce) cans artichoke hearts, drained
1/2 cup chopped celery
1/4 cup chopped green onions
1/2 cup mayonnaise
salt and pepper to taste
crumbled crisp-cooked bacon

Squeeze the excess moisture from the artichokes and finely chop. Combine the artichokes, celery and green onions in a bowl and mix well. Stir in the mayonnaise, salt and pepper. Sprinkle with bacon. This is a most versatile dish. Serve as a salad stuffed into a fresh tomato half, as a spread on turkey or ham sandwiches, as an appetizer with crackers, as a dressing for tomato aspic, or as an accompaniment to fish, especially salmon.

MISS EMMA PORTER'S MAYONNAISE

MAKES 2 CUPS

2 egg yolks
1/4 of 1 egg white
2 tablespoons lemon juice
1/2 teaspoon salt
1/4 teaspoon red pepper
2 cups vegetable oil
1 teaspoon boiling water

Whisk the egg yolks, egg white, 1 tablespoon of the lemon juice, salt and red pepper in a bowl. Add 1 cup of the oil gradually, whisking constantly until the mixture begins to thicken. Add the remaining 1 tablespoon lemon juice and remaining oil gradually, whisking constantly until thickened. Whisk in the boiling water. Store, covered, in the refrigerator. To avoid raw eggs that may carry salmonella, we suggest using an equivalent amount of pasteurized egg substitute.

CUCUMBER AND DILL SAUCE

MAKES 2 CUPS

1 cup sour cream
1 cucumber, peeled, seeded and chopped
3 tablespoons chopped fresh dill weed or watercress
1/4 teaspoon each salt and sugar
1/4 teaspoon wine vinegar

Combine all the ingredients in a bowl and mix well. Serve with salmon or any baked or broiled fish. You may substitute a mixture of 1/2 cup yogurt and 1/2 cup sour cream for the sour cream.

SALSA VERDE

MAKES 1 TO 1 1/2 CUPS

1 (3-inch) piece French bread, crust removed
1 1/4 cups flat-leaf parsley leaves
1 tablespoon drained capers
3 anchovy fillets
2 tablespoons minced onion
1 garlic clove, minced
2 1/2 teaspoons red wine vinegar
1/2 teaspoon salt
freshly ground pepper to taste
1/2 cup olive oil

Soak the bread in a small amount of water to moisten; squeeze dry. Combine with the next 8 ingredients in a blender. Process until puréed. Add the olive oil gradually, processing constantly until blended. Store, covered, in the refrigerator.

135

Although James and Sarah Polk had no children of their own, they became "adoptive" parents to a number of younger siblings, nieces, and nephews. They surrounded themselves with these young people their entire lives. Along with the joys of family, there were also many sorrows. Two of Sarah's closest nieces both died within weeks of one another while giving birth to their first children. One of James's brothers, Samuel Polk, whom James and Sarah favored, died of tuberculosis at age twenty-one. Sending letters describing his declining health, the dying young man assured Sarah that her kindness was "more the kindness of a Mother than a Sister."

The Polk Home was built in 1816 by President Polk's father, Samuel. The Federal-style house was the first brick residence built in Columbia and is the only home that remains that James K. Polk lived in. Today it is filled with objects that James and Sarah Polk collected throughout their illustrious and interesting lives.

From the Hearth

GEORGIA'S BISCUITS

MAKES 4 DOZEN

1 cup vegetable shortening
6 cups self-rising flour
2 cups (or more) buttermilk

Cut the shortening into the self-rising flour in a bowl until crumbly. Add the buttermilk gradually and mix until a soft dough forms. Knead the dough lightly on a lightly floured surface. Roll 1/2 inch thick and cut into rounds with a biscuit cutter.

Arrange the rounds 2 inches apart on an ungreased baking sheet. Place the baking sheet on the middle oven rack. Bake at 400 degrees for 15 to 18 minutes or until light brown. Serve immediately. A preheated oven is recommended.

GRANNY'S BISCUITS

MAKES 4 DOZEN

3 to 4 cups self-rising flour
3 cups whipping cream

Combine the self-rising flour and whipping cream in a bowl and mix with a wooden spoon until a soft dough forms. Knead on a lightly floured surface. Roll 1/2 inch thick and cut into squares or rounds. Arrange the squares or rounds on a cast-iron baker or baking sheet. Bake on the middle oven rack at 415 degrees for 15 minutes or until light brown. Serve immediately.

HERB CRESCENT ROLLS

MAKES 20

2 cups crushed crisp rice cereal
1 tablespoon caraway seeds
1 tablespoon sesame seeds
1 teaspoon seasoned salt, or to taste
10 canned refrigerator biscuits
6 tablespoons margarine, melted

Line a baking sheet with heavy-duty foil and spray lightly with nonstick cooking spray. Combine the cereal, caraway seeds, sesame seeds and seasoned salt in a bowl and mix well. Cut each biscuit horizontally into halves.

Dip each biscuit half into the melted margarine and coat with the cereal mixture. Arrange the biscuit halves in a single layer on the prepared baking sheet. Bake at 400 degrees for 8 to 11 minutes or until puffed and golden brown. A preheated oven is recommended.

SUNRISE MUFFINS
MAKES 2 DOZEN

2 cups flour
1 1/2 cups sugar
2 teaspoons baking powder
2 teaspoons cinnamon
1/2 teaspoon salt
2 cups grated carrots
1 cup vegetable oil
3 eggs, beaten
1 teaspoon vanilla extract
1/2 cup chopped dates
1/2 cup flaked coconut
1/2 cup chopped pecans

Sift the flour, sugar, baking powder, cinnamon and salt into a bowl and mix well. Stir in the carrots, oil, eggs and vanilla. Fold in the dates, coconut and pecans. Fill greased muffin cups 2/3 full.

Bake at 375 degrees for 25 minutes or just until the muffins spring back when lightly touched. You may freeze for future use. A preheated oven is recommended.

Sarah Polk's time at Salem Academy in North Carolina was bittersweet. Given a gold coin called a louis d'or by her father (that she kept for her entire life), she, her sister Susan, brother Anderson, and a servant took the five-hundred-mile journey on horseback to North Carolina. She seemed to enjoy and profit from her time at the academy, but after just one year, she was called home by the death of her father. In his will he provided liberally for his wife and children, Sarah receiving one quarter of the contents of the family home and nearly one quarter of his monetary estate.

POPOVERS

MAKES 12

1 cup milk
1 cup flour
4 extra-large eggs
1 teaspoon salt
2 tablespoons unsalted butter, melted

Whisk the milk, flour, eggs and salt in a 4-cup measure. Whisk in the unsalted butter; the batter will be lumpy. Let stand for 5 minutes. Pour the batter into 12 miniature or 1/4-cup popover cups sprayed with nonstick cooking spray.

Bake on the middle oven rack at 400 degrees for 25 to 30 minutes or until brown. Cool in pan for 1 minute. Remove the popovers to a wire rack and pierce each popover to allow the steam to escape. Serve immediately. You may prepare the batter 1 day in advance and store, covered, in the refrigerator; the batter does not have to be returned to room temperature to proceed with the recipe. Muffin cups are not recommended for this recipe. A preheated oven is recommended.

SAVORY SCONES

MAKES 2 DOZEN

SCONES

4 cups flour
2 tablespoons baking powder
1 1/2 teaspoons salt
1/2 cup (1 stick) unsalted butter,
sliced and chilled
6 ounces extra-sharp Cheddar
cheese, shredded
1 cup milk
2/3 cup heavy cream

HONEY-MUSTARD BUTTER AND ASSEMBLY

1/2 cup (1 stick) unsalted butter, softened
3 tablespoons clover honey
3 tablespoons coarse-grain mustard
sliced cooked ham

For the scones, sift the flour, baking powder and salt into a large bowl. Cut in the butter until crumbly. Stir in the cheese with a fork. Add the milk and heavy cream and mix just until moistened. Knead on a lightly floured surface until the mixture forms a dough. Roll the dough into a 12-inch round, 1/2 inch thick. Cut into 2-inch rounds with a biscuit cutter, reserving the scraps. Reroll and cut the reserved scraps. Arrange the rounds on a baking sheet. Bake at 425 degrees for 12 minutes. Cool on the baking sheet for 2 minutes.

For the butter, mix the unsalted butter, honey and mustard in a bowl until blended.

To serve, split the scones and spread the cut sides with the butter. Fill with sliced ham. A preheated oven is recommended.

DANISH ALMOND APPLE PUFFS

SERVES 10 TO 12

PASTRY
1 cup flour
2 tablespoons sugar
1/2 cup (1 stick) butter
2 tablespoons water

APPLE FILLING
1 cup water
1/2 cup (1 stick) butter
1 teaspoon sugar
1 teaspoon almond extract
1 cup flour
4 eggs
1 cooking apple, peeled and chopped
1 tablespoon sugar
1/3 cup sliced almonds
2 tablespoons confectioners' sugar

For the pastry, mix the flour and sugar in a bowl. Cut in the butter until crumbly. Sprinkle with the water and mix well with a fork. Roll the pastry into a ball and divide into 2 equal portions. Pat each portion into a 3×12-inch strip on a lightly floured surface. Arrange the strips 3 inches apart on an ungreased baking sheet.

For the filling, bring the water and butter to a boil in a saucepan, stirring occasionally. Remove from the heat. Stir in the flavoring and 1 teaspoon sugar. Add the flour and beat until smooth with a heavy spoon. Beat in the eggs 1 at a time. Spread half the mixture over each dough strip. Toss the apple, 1 tablespoon sugar and almonds in a bowl. Spread half the apple mixture over each strip. Bake at 350 degrees for 1 hour; do not underbake. Sprinkle with the confectioners' sugar. A preheated oven is recommended.

141

Sarah Polk enjoyed music throughout her entire life. A pianoforte purchased by her father that Sarah grew up playing in Murfreesboro still exists, as does a music book written in her own hand while a student at the Moravian Academy in Salem, North Carolina. Sarah, while living in Washington as a congressman's wife, tried to continue her piano lessons, but found the continuous rounds of parties, dinners, and balls too demanding of her time, and she was forced to give up her musical pursuits.

BLUEBERRY-STUFFED FRENCH TOAST

SERVES 9

1 (16-ounce) loaf dry French bread
11 ounces cream cheese, softened
1¹/2 cups fresh blueberries
2 cups milk
12 eggs
1 cup maple syrup
1/8 teaspoon cinnamon

Cut the loaf into eighteen 1-inch slices. Arrange 9 of the slices in a single layer in a lightly greased 9×13-inch baking dish. Spread the cream cheese over the bread slices and sprinkle with the blueberries. Top with the remaining 9 slices of bread.

Whisk the milk, eggs, maple syrup and cinnamon in a bowl until blended. Pour the milk mixture over the prepared layers. Chill, covered, for 8 hours. Let stand at room temperature for 30 minutes. Bake at 350 degrees for 20 minutes; cover with foil. Bake for 25 minutes longer. Serve with additional hot maple syrup. A preheated oven is recommended.

CARROT BREAD

MAKES 2 LOAVES

BREAD

2 cups flour
1¹/2 cups sugar
2 teaspoons baking soda
2 teaspoons cinnamon
1 teaspoon ground cloves
1/2 teaspoon salt
1¹/2 cups vegetable oil
2 tablespoons vanilla extract
3 eggs
2 cups grated carrots

CREAM CHEESE SPREAD

3 ounces cream cheese, softened
confectioners' sugar to taste

For the bread, sift the flour, sugar, baking soda, cinnamon, cloves and salt into a large mixing bowl and mix well. Stir in the oil, vanilla and eggs. Beat at medium speed until blended, scraping the bowl occasionally. Fold in the carrots. Spoon the batter into 2 greased 4×8-inch loaf pans. Bake at 300 degrees for 1 hour or until the loaves test done. Cool in pan for 10 minutes. Remove to a wire rack to cool completely.

For the spread, process the cream cheese and confectioners' sugar in a food processor until smooth. Serve with the bread. Store leftover spread in the refrigerator. A preheated oven is recommended.

BAY'S CORN BREAD

S E R V E S   8

3 tablespoons vegetable oil
2 cups white cornmeal
1 teaspoon baking soda
1 teaspoon baking powder
1 teaspoon salt
2 eggs
2 cups buttermilk
1/4 cup bacon drippings or vegetable oil

Pour the oil into a cast-iron skillet. Place the skillet in the upper third of the oven while preheating the oven to 400 degrees; the skillet must be very hot. Mix the cornmeal, baking soda, baking powder and salt in a bowl.

Whisk the eggs in a bowl until blended. Stir in the cornmeal mixture, buttermilk and bacon drippings. Remove the hot skillet from the oven and tilt the skillet to ensure even coverage. Discard all but 1 tablespoon of the oil. Pour the batter into the hot skillet. Bake for 30 to 35 minutes or until light brown and crisp. Invert the corn bread onto a wire rack. You may bake the corn bread in muffin cups or in a breadstick pan. Freeze baked corn bread for future use if desired. A preheated oven is recommended.

CORNELIA'S CORN LIGHT BREAD

M A K E S   1   L O A F

1 1/2 cups self-rising cornmeal
1/2 cup flour
1/2 cup sugar
1/8 teaspoon salt
1/8 teaspoon baking powder
1/4 cup shortening
2 cups buttermilk

Combine the self-rising cornmeal, flour, sugar, salt, baking powder, shortening and buttermilk in the order listed in a bowl and mix well. Spoon the batter into a 5×9-inch loaf pan. Let stand to rise for 10 minutes if desired.

Bake at 350 degrees for 50 to 60 minutes or until the loaf tests done. Cool in the pan for 10 minutes. Remove to a wire rack. A preheated oven is recommended.

EASY DILL BEER BREAD

MAKES 1 LOAF

3 cups self-rising flour
3 tablespoons light brown sugar
1 tablespoon dill weed
1 (12-ounce) can beer
1/4 cup (1/2 stick) unsalted butter, melted
1 to 2 tablespoons unsalted butter, softened

Mix the self-rising flour, brown sugar and dill weed in a bowl. Stir in the beer. Spoon the batter into a buttered 5×9-inch loaf pan. Drizzle with 1/4 cup melted unsalted butter.

Bake at 375 degrees for 50 to 55 minutes or until the loaf sounds hollow when lightly tapped. Spread the top with 1 to 2 tablespoons softened unsalted butter. Cool in pan for 10 minutes. Remove to a wire rack. You may slice the loaf, spread the slices with butter, wrap in foil and freeze for future use. Reheat before serving. A preheated oven is recommended.

BEST-EVER ZUCCHINI BREAD

MAKES 2 LOAVES

2 cups sifted flour
2 teaspoons baking soda
2 teaspoons cinnamon
1 teaspoon salt
1/8 teaspoon baking powder
3 eggs
1 1/2 cups sugar
1 cup vegetable oil
2 teaspoons vanilla extract
2 cups grated zucchini
1/2 cup chopped nuts

Combine the flour, baking soda, cinnamon, salt and baking powder in a bowl and mix well. Beat the eggs in a mixing bowl until blended. Add the sugar, oil and vanilla to the eggs and beat until smooth. Beat in the flour mixture. Stir in the zucchini and nuts.

Spoon the batter into 2 greased 4×8-inch loaf pans. Bake at 325 degrees for 1 hour. Cool in pans for 10 minutes. Remove to a wire rack to cool completely. A preheated oven is recommended.

ALPINE BRAIDED BREAD
MAKES 2 LOAVES

1 envelope dry yeast
1¹/₂ cups milk, heated
¹/₂ cup sugar
1¹/₂ teaspoons salt
4¹/₂ cups (about) bread flour
¹/₄ cup vegetable oil

Sprinkle the yeast over the milk in a mixing bowl. Stir in the sugar and salt. Proof for 5 minutes. Add half the bread flour and the oil to the yeast mixture and beat until smooth. Add the remaining flour and mix until blended. Knead the dough until smooth and elastic, adding additional flour as needed for an easily handled dough.

Place the dough in a greased bowl and turn to coat. Let rise, covered with waxed paper, for 1 hour or until doubled in bulk. Divide the dough into 2 equal portions. Cut each portion into 3 equal pieces. Roll each piece into a rope. Shape 3 of the ropes into a braid on a lightly greased baking sheet and seal the ends. Repeat the process with the remaining 3 ropes. Bake at 350 degrees for 30 minutes or until the loaves test done. Remove to a wire rack to cool. A preheated oven is recommended.

The Tennessee State Legislature was meeting in Murfreesboro in 1819 when twenty-four-year-old James K. Polk was elected Clerk of the Senate. James spent much of his free time with a local resident who would become his closest personal and political confidante. Sixteen-year-old Sarah Childress shared her future husband's Democratic ideals and encouraged his political aspirations. Some historians have speculated that James might have met Sarah earlier. He briefly attended Bradley Academy in Murfreesboro in 1815 and probably knew Sarah's brother Anderson at the University of North Carolina.

LIGHT-AS-A-FEATHER ITALIAN BREAD
MAKES 2 LOAVES

1 cup warm (100 to 115 degrees) water
2 envelopes dry yeast
1 tablespoon sugar
1/3 cup butter or margarine, cut into pieces
3/4 cup hot water

2 teaspoons salt
4 1/2 to 5 1/2 cups all-purpose flour or bread flour
butter, softened
cornmeal
1 egg white, lightly beaten

Combine the warm water, yeast and sugar in a bowl. Let stand until the mixture swells and becomes bubbly. Melt 1/3 cup butter in the hot water. Cool to lukewarm. Add the salt to the butter mixture and mix well. Stir the butter mixture into the yeast mixture.

Add the flour 1 cup at a time to the yeast mixture, stirring vigorously with a wooden spoon until the dough begins to pull from the side of the bowl. Turn the dough onto a lightly floured surface. Knead for 2 to 4 minutes, adding flour as needed. Let rest for 5 to 6 minutes.

Divide the dough into 2 equal portions. Roll each portion into an 8×12-inch rectangle on a lightly floured surface. Starting at the wide end, roll each rectangle tightly, sealing the seams as you roll. Brush a large baking sheet with butter and sprinkle with cornmeal. Arrange the loaves on the prepared baking sheet.

Let rise, covered with a tea towel, in a warm place for 50 to 60 minutes. Brush with the egg white. Bake at 375 degrees for 25 to 35 minutes or until the loaves sound hollow when lightly tapped and are golden brown in color. Remove the loaves to a wire rack to cool. A preheated oven is recommended.

CINNAMON ROLLS

MAKES 12 TO 14

1/4 cup warm (110 degrees) water
1 teaspoon sugar
1 envelope dry yeast
2 1/2 to 3 cups flour
3/4 cup milk, heated
1/4 cup each sugar and shortening
1 egg, lightly beaten
1 teaspoon salt
1/4 cup (1/2 stick) butter, softened
1/2 cup sugar
2 teaspoons cinnamon
2 cups confectioners' sugar
3 to 4 tablespoons milk
1/4 teaspoon vanilla extract

Mix the warm water, 1 teaspoon sugar and yeast. Let stand for 5 minutes. Combine with 1 3/4 cups of the flour, warm milk, 1/4 cup sugar, shortening, egg and salt in a mixing bowl. Beat until blended. Add enough of the remaining flour to make a soft dough.

Knead on a lightly floured surface for 5 minutes or until smooth and elastic. Place in a greased bowl, turning to coat the surface. Let rise, covered, in a warm place for 1 1/2 hours or until doubled in bulk. Punch the dough down. Let rise, covered, in a warm place free from drafts for 30 minutes or until doubled in bulk. Roll into a 9×15-inch rectangle on a lightly floured surface. Spread with the butter and sprinkle with a mixture of 1/2 cup sugar and the cinnamon. Roll as for a jelly roll. Cut into 1-inch slices. Arrange cut side up in a lightly greased 9×13-inch baking pan. Let rise, covered, in a warm place for 30 minutes or until doubled in bulk. Bake at 375 degrees for 17 minutes or until the rolls test done. Mix the confectioners' sugar, milk and vanilla in a bowl. Drizzle over the hot rolls. A preheated oven is recommended.

Born on the Tennessee frontier on September 4, 1803, Sarah Childress was the third child of Joel and Elizabeth Childress of Rutherford County. Joel was a successful merchant, tavern keeper, and planter who befriended many of early Tennessee's political leaders. Visitors to the Childress home and to Joel's tavern in Murfreesboro included Judge John Overton, Governor Joseph McMinn, and General Andrew Jackson. Joel provided the full dress uniform that General Jackson took to New Orleans during the War of 1812. Surrounded by her father's influential acquaintances, young Sarah acquired political knowledge and interests long before she married James K. Polk.

This silk and wool embroidery work was completed by fourteen-year-old Sarah Childress at Salem Academy in North Carolina. It is considered one of the best surviving examples of 19th-century schoolgirl art. The tomb scene may have influenced architect William Strickland when he designed James K. Polk's tomb in 1849.

Sweet Temptations

ASHWOOD APPLE LAYER CAKE

S E R V E S   1 2

CAKE

3 cups flour
1¹/2 teaspoons baking soda
¹/2 teaspoon salt
3 cups grated peeled Granny
Smith apples

1 teaspoon grated lemon zest
2 cups sugar
1¹/2 cups vegetable oil
2 eggs, beaten
¹/2 cup chopped walnuts

EASY CARAMEL ICING

1 cup (2 sticks) butter
2 cups packed dark brown sugar

¹/2 cup milk
4 cups sifted confectioners' sugar

For the cake, grease and flour three 9-inch cake pans. Mix the flour, baking soda and salt in a bowl. Toss the apples with the lemon zest in a bowl. Combine the sugar, oil and eggs in a bowl and mix until blended. Add the dry ingredients and stir until mixed. Stir in the apple mixture and walnuts.

Spoon the batter into the prepared pans. Bake at 350 degrees for 25 to 35 minutes or until the layers spring back when lightly touched. Cool in pans for 10 minutes. Remove to a wire rack to cool completely.

For the icing, melt the butter in a heavy 2-quart saucepan. Stir in the brown sugar. Bring to a boil. Boil for 2 minutes, stirring constantly; this timing is very important. Remove from the heat and stir in the milk carefully. Cool to lukewarm. Add the confectioners' sugar and beat with a whisk or spoon until smooth and of a spreading consistency. Immediately spread the icing between the layers and over the top and side of the cake. If the icing becomes too thick, add a little hot water. The icing may be frozen for future use. Reheat before using, adding water as needed for the desired consistency. A preheated oven is recommended.

FRONT PORCH CHOCOLATE CAKE
SERVES 12

CAKE

3 cups sugar

2 1/2 cups flour

1 cup plus 2 tablespoons baking cocoa

2 1/4 teaspoons baking soda

2 1/4 teaspoons baking powder

1 1/2 teaspoons salt

3 eggs

1 1/2 cups milk

3/4 cup vegetable oil

1 tablespoon vanilla extract

1 1/2 cups boiling water

CHOCOLATE CREAM CHEESE ICING

8 ounces cream cheese, softened

1/2 cup (1 stick) butter, softened

1 teaspoon vanilla extract

4 cups confectioners' sugar

1/2 cup baking cocoa

For the cake, grease three 9-inch cake pans or spray with nonstick cooking spray. Combine the sugar, flour, baking cocoa, baking soda, baking powder and salt in a mixing bowl and mix well. Add the eggs 1 at a time and beat at low speed until blended. Add the milk, oil and vanilla gradually, beating constantly at medium speed until smooth. Add the boiling water gradually and beat at low speed until mixed; the batter will be very thin.

Pour the batter into the prepared cake pans. Bake at 350 degrees for 20 to 30 minutes or until the layers test done. Cool in the pans. Remove the layers and wrap in plastic wrap. Freeze until firm.

For the icing, beat the cream cheese and butter in a mixing bowl until light and fluffy, scraping the bowl occasionally. Add the vanilla and beat until blended. Add the confectioners' sugar and baking cocoa gradually and beat at medium speed until smooth and of a spreading consistency. Spread the icing between the layers and over the top and side of the cake. Garnish with white and dark chocolate curls if desired. A preheated oven is recommended.

CHOCOLATE CHIP CAKE

SERVES 12 TO 16

1 (2-layer) package yellow cake mix
1 (4-ounce) package chocolate instant pudding mix
1 cup sour cream
1/2 cup vegetable oil
4 eggs
2 cups (12 ounces) chocolate chips
1/2 cup (1 stick) butter
3 tablespoons milk
3 tablespoons baking cocoa
1/2 (1-pound) package (or more) confectioners' sugar
1/2 teaspoon vanilla extract

Combine the cake mix, pudding mix, sour cream, oil and eggs in a mixing bowl. Beat until blended, scraping the bowl occasionally. Fold in the chocolate chips. Spoon the batter into a bundt pan sprayed with nonstick cooking spray. Bake at 350 degrees for 45 minutes. Cool in the pan for 10 minutes. Invert onto a cake plate.

Combine the butter, milk and baking cocoa in a saucepan. Bring to a boil, stirring frequently. Remove from the heat. Add the confectioners' sugar and vanilla and beat until of a glaze consistency, adding additional confectioners' sugar if desired for a thicker consistency. Drizzle the warm glaze over the cake and into the center well. A preheated oven is recommended.

DOBOSCHE TORTE

SERVES 10 TO 12

2 (8-ounce) milk chocolate candy bars, broken
1/2 cup strong coffee
1/4 cup Cognac or other brandy
16 ounces frozen whipped topping, thawed
1 round angel food cake

Combine the candy bars, coffee and liqueur in a 2-quart microwave-safe bowl. Microwave on Medium for 5 to 6 minutes or until the chocolate melts; stir. Let stand until cool. Fold in the whipped topping.

Cut the cake horizontally into 3 or 4 layers. Spread the whipped topping mixture between the layers and over the top and side of the cake. Store, covered, in the refrigerator.

PLANTATION CAKE

S E R V E S   1 2

CAKE

1 (2-layer) package yellow cake mix
1 (4-ounce) package vanilla instant pudding mix
1 1/3 cups water
1/2 cup (1 stick) margarine, softened
4 eggs
1 cup (6 ounces) semisweet chocolate chips, melted
1 teaspoon vanilla extract
1 cup pecans, chopped
2/3 cup (4 ounces) semisweet chocolate chips

CREAM CHEESE FROSTING

8 ounces cream cheese, softened
1/4 cup (1/2 stick) margarine, softened
4 cups confectioners' sugar
1 teaspoon vanilla extract

For the cake, mix the cake mix and pudding mix in a mixing bowl. Add the water and margarine. Beat just until moistened. Add the eggs 1 at a time, beating well after each addition. Stir in the melted chocolate chips.

Beat at high speed for 2 minutes, scraping the bowl occasionally. Stir in the vanilla. Spoon the batter into three 8-inch cake pans sprayed with nonstick cooking spray. Toss the pecans and 2/3 cup chocolate chips in a bowl. Sprinkle 1/3 of the pecan mixture over the top of each layer. Bake at 350 degrees for 35 to 40 minutes or until the layers test done. Cool in pans for 10 minutes. Remove to a wire rack to cool completely.

For the frosting, beat the cream cheese and margarine in a mixing bowl until light and fluffy. Add the confectioners' sugar and vanilla and beat until smooth, scraping the bowl occasionally. Spread the frosting between the layers and over the side of the cake. A preheated oven is recommended.

*T*wenty-year-old Sarah Childress married twenty-eight-year-old state legislator James K. Polk on New Year's Day 1824. The country wedding at the bride's home near Murfreesboro attracted personal and political friends from throughout Middle Tennessee. The ceremony was followed by four days of dinners and parties in Murfreesboro. The newlyweds then traveled to the groom's hometown, Columbia, for another round of celebratory activities. After meeting Sarah for the first time, a Polk family friend observed that "her eyes looked as if she had a great deal of spice."

OATMEAL CAKE

S E R V E S   1 5

CAKE

1¼ cups boiling water
1 cup rolled oats
1⅓ cups flour, sifted
1 teaspoon baking soda
1 teaspoon cinnamon
½ cup (1 stick) butter or margarine,
softened

1 cup packed dark brown sugar
1 cup sugar
2 eggs
1 teaspoon vanilla extract

COCONUT TOPPING

1 (3-ounce) can coconut flakes
1 cup chopped pecans
⅔ cup packed dark brown sugar

¼ cup cream
3 tablespoons butter, melted
1 egg, lightly beaten

For the cake, pour the boiling water over the oats in a heatproof bowl. Let stand for 20 minutes. Sift the flour, baking soda and cinnamon together. Beat the butter, brown sugar and sugar in a mixing bowl until creamy. Add the creamed mixture to the oats mixture and mix well. Add the eggs and vanilla and mix well. Fold in the dry ingredients. Spoon the batter into a 9×13-inch cake pan sprayed with nonstick cooking spray. Bake at 350 degrees for 45 minutes.

For the topping, combine the coconut, pecans, brown sugar, cream, butter and egg in a bowl and mix well. Spread the topping over the hot cake. Bake for 10 minutes longer. Cool in the pan on a wire rack. A preheated oven is recommended.

POUND CAKE

S E R V E S   1 6

---

3 cups flour
3 cups sugar
1 cup (2 sticks) butter
6 eggs
1 cup heavy cream
1/2 teaspoon almond extract
1/2 teaspoon vanilla extract

Sift the flour twice. Beat the sugar and butter in a mixing bowl until creamy, scraping the bowl occasionally. Add the eggs 1 at a time, beating for 1 minute after each addition. Add the flour alternately with the heavy cream, beginning and ending with the flour and beating well after each addition. Stir in the flavorings.

Spoon the batter into a buttered and floured tube pan. Place the pan in a cold oven. Bake at 300 degrees for 1 1/2 hours. Cool in the pan for 10 minutes. Remove to a wire rack to cool completely.

Sarah Polk was a great asset to her husband's career. At different times in their illustrious lives, Sarah played the part of private secretary, campaign manager, official correspondent, and confidante. James K. Polk was a very private person and tended to keep his own counsel. Always listening to Cabinet members, he nevertheless reserved the final decision for himself. Sarah was the only one who completely knew his mind. A New York newspaper labeled her "a most auspicious domestic influence, and the President's guardian angel." The President put it more plainly when he stated, "None but Sarah knew so intimately my private affairs."

PRUNE CAKE WITH CARAMEL GLAZE
SERVES 15

CAKE

2 cups flour	1 cup vegetable oil
1 teaspoon salt	1 cup buttermilk
1 teaspoon baking soda	2 eggs
1 teaspoon allspice	1 cup chopped prunes
1 1/2 cups sugar	1 cup chopped pecans

CARAMEL GLAZE

3 tablespoons butter	3 tablespoons heavy cream
3 tablespoons light brown sugar	1/2 teaspoon vanilla extract
3 tablespoons sugar	

For the cake, mix the flour, salt, baking soda and allspice together. Beat the sugar, oil, buttermilk and eggs in a mixing bowl until smooth. Fold in the flour mixture. Stir in the prunes and pecans. Spoon the batter into a 9×9-inch cake pan or 9×13-inch cake pan sprayed with nonstick cooking spray. Bake at 325 degrees for 40 minutes or until the cake tests done. Cool in the pan on a wire rack.

For the glaze, combine the butter, brown sugar, sugar, heavy cream and vanilla in a saucepan. Bring to a boil over medium heat, stirring frequently. Boil for 1 minute, stirring frequently. Remove from the heat. Cool to a drizzling consistency. Drizzle the glaze over the cake. A preheated oven is recommended.

YUM RUM CAKE

SERVES 15

CAKE

1/2 to 1 cup chopped pecans
1 (2-layer) package yellow cake mix
1/2 cup vegetable oil
1/2 cup water
1/2 cup dark rum
4 eggs

RUM GLAZE

1 cup sugar
1/2 cup (1 stick) butter
1/2 cup dark rum
1/4 cup water

For the cake, grease and flour a bundt pan. Sprinkle the pecans over the bottom of the prepared pan. Combine the cake mix, oil, water, rum and eggs in a mixing bowl. Beat until blended, scraping the bowl occasionally. Spoon the batter into the prepared pan. Bake at 350 degrees for 30 minutes. Cool in the pan for 10 minutes. Remove to a cake plate.

For the glaze, combine the sugar, butter, rum and water in a microwave-safe bowl. Microwave for 1 minute; stir. Drizzle the glaze over the warm cake. A preheated oven is recommended.

While James K. Polk was a member of Congress for fourteen years, he and Sarah lived in rented rooms in boardinghouses. They kept private sleeping quarters, but shared an open parlor and dining area with other Congressmen and their wives. It was during these years of close-quarters living that Sarah became so politically astute and an advisor to her husband. When Polk became Speaker of the House, his increased status required them to move into private quarters, where Sarah would hone the skill of entertaining and conversing with the political elite.

CHOCOLATE CAPPUCCINO CHEESECAKE

SERVES 16

CRUST

1 cup chocolate wafer crumbs
2 tablespoons sugar

1/4 teaspoon cinnamon
1/4 cup (1/2 stick) butter, softened

CHOCOLATE FILLING

2 teaspoons instant espresso
powder
1/4 cup hot water
24 ounces cream cheese, softened
1 cup sugar
3 eggs

8 ounces semisweet chocolate
2 tablespoons whipping cream
1 cup sour cream
1/4 cup coffee liqueur
2 teaspoons vanilla extract
1/4 teaspoon salt

CHOCOLATE LEAVES AND ASSEMBLY

melted semisweet chocolate
1 cup whipping cream

2 tablespoons confectioners' sugar
2 tablespoons coffee liqueur

For the crust, combine the wafer crumbs, sugar and cinnamon in a bowl and mix well. Add the butter and mix well. Pat the crumb mixture over the bottom of a buttered 9-inch springform pan.

For the filling, dissolve the espresso powder in the hot water in a heatproof bowl. Beat the cream cheese in a mixing bowl until smooth. Add the sugar gradually and beat until blended. Add the eggs 1 at a time and beat at low speed until smooth.

Combine the chocolate and whipping cream in a double boiler over boiling water. Heat until blended, stirring frequently. Add the chocolate mixture to the cream cheese mixture and beat until blended. Beat in the coffee, sour cream, liqueur, vanilla and salt until smooth. Spoon the batter into the prepared pan. Bake on the center oven rack at 350 degrees for 45 minutes. Chill, covered, for 12 hours.

For the chocolate leaves, brush 1 side of real leaves with melted chocolate. Freeze until firm. Peel off the real leaves and discard. Freeze the chocolate leaves until just before serving.

To serve, beat the whipping cream in a mixing bowl until soft peaks form. Add the confectioners' sugar and liqueur and mix well. Cut the cheesecake into 16 wedges and top each with a dollop of the flavored whipped cream and chocolate leaves. A preheated oven is recommended.

AMARETTO MOUSSE CAKE

SERVES 10 TO 12

CRUST

2 cups graham cracker crumbs
1/2 cup chopped almonds
1/3 cup sugar
1/2 cup (1 stick) margarine, softened

AMARETTO FILLING

24 ounces cream cheese, softened
2/3 cup sugar
1 cup sour cream
1/2 cup amaretto
4 eggs

For the crust, combine the graham cracker crumbs, almonds and sugar in a bowl and mix well. Add the margarine and mix well. Press the crumb mixture over the bottom of an ungreased 8-inch springform pan.

For the filling, beat the cream cheese and sugar in a mixing bowl until smooth. Add the sour cream and liqueur and beat until blended. Add the eggs. Beat at low speed just until blended. Spoon the cream cheese mixture into the prepared pan. Bake at 350 degrees for 50 to 60 minutes or until the edge is slightly puffed and the center appears moist. Turn off the oven.

Let the cheesecake stand in the oven with the door ajar for 30 minutes. Cool in the pan on a wire rack for 1 hour. Chill, covered, for 3 hours or longer or freeze for future use. A preheated oven is recommended.

The Polks were painted by some of the most important American artists, G. P. A. Healy and Thomas Sully among them. The first portraits of them were painted by Ralph E. W. Earl in Washington, D.C. Sarah Polk later reminisced, "The Tennesseans who were assembled one evening in the parlor proposed that they should have their portraits painted by Mr. Earl, and this proposition was soon carried into effect." Polk was a thirty-four-year-old congressman at the time, Sarah just twenty-six. Sarah's portrait shows a lovely, fashionable young woman with dark hair piled atop her head, dark, piercing eyes, and sharp features that are characteristic of Earl's work.

STRAWBERRY-GLAZED CHEESECAKE

SERVES 12 TO 16

CRUST

3/4 cup coarsely ground walnuts
3/4 cup fine graham cracker crumbs

3 tablespoons butter, melted

CREAM CHEESE FILLING

32 ounces cream cheese, softened
1 1/4 cups sugar
4 eggs

1 tablespoon fresh lemon juice
2 teaspoons vanilla extract

SOUR CREAM TOPPING

2 cups sour cream
1/4 cup sugar

1 teaspoon vanilla extract

STRAWBERRY GLAZE AND ASSEMBLY

1 (12-ounce) jar red raspberry jelly
1 tablespoon cornstarch
1/4 cup Grand Marnier or Cointreau

1/4 cup water
1 quart medium strawberries

For the crust, combine the walnuts, graham cracker crumbs and butter in a bowl and mix well. Pat the crumb mixture over the bottom of a lightly buttered 9-inch springform pan.

For the filling, beat the cream cheese in a mixing bowl until smooth. Add the sugar, eggs, lemon juice and vanilla. Beat until blended, scraping the bowl occasionally. Spoon the filling into the prepared pan. Bake at 350 degrees for 55 minutes. Cool for 15 minutes. Maintain the oven temperature.

For the topping, combine the sour cream, sugar and vanilla in a bowl and mix well. Spread the topping over the baked layer to within 1/2 inch of the edge. Bake for 10 minutes longer. Cool in the pan on a wire rack. Chill, covered, for 24 hours or preferably for 2 to 3 days.

For the glaze, combine a small amount of the jelly with the cornstarch in a saucepan and mix well. Stir in the remaining jelly, liqueur and water. Cook over medium heat for 5 minutes or until thickened and clear, stirring frequently. Let stand until lukewarm.

To serve, run a sharp knife around the edge of the cheesecake and remove the side of the pan. Arrange the strawberries pointed ends up in a decorative pattern over the top of the cheesecake. Spoon the glaze over the strawberries, allowing some of the glaze to drizzle down the side of the cheesecake. Chill until set. A preheated oven is recommended.

DOUBLE BERRY SHORTCAKES

SERVES 8

SHORTCAKES

1 3/4 cups flour	1 teaspoon grated lemon zest
5 tablespoons sugar	1/4 cup (1/2 stick) butter, chilled
1 teaspoon baking powder	1 cup plus 1 tablespoon half-and-half
1/4 teaspoon salt	1 egg, lightly beaten

BERRY FILLING

2 pints fresh strawberries, cut into halves	1/2 cup sugar
1 pint blueberries	1 tablespoon lemon juice

WHIPPED CREAM AND ASSEMBLY

2 cups whipping cream	1 teaspoon vanilla extract
1 tablespoon sugar	

For the shortcakes, sift the flour, sugar, baking powder and salt into a bowl and mix well. Stir in the lemon zest. Place the flour mixture in a food processor and add the butter. Process until crumbly. Add 1 cup of the half-and-half to the crumb mixture and process until mixed.

Pat the dough 3/8 inch thick on a lightly floured surface. Cut into rounds with a 3-inch biscuit cutter. Arrange the rounds on a baking sheet. Mix the remaining 1 tablespoon half-and-half and egg in a bowl. Brush the egg mixture over the rounds. Bake at 425 degrees for 15 minutes. Cool on the baking sheet for 2 minutes. Remove to a wire rack to cool completely. For variety, use heart cookie cutters for Valentine's Day and star cookie cutters for the Fourth of July.

For the filling, toss the strawberries, blueberries, sugar and lemon juice in a bowl. Chill, covered, in the refrigerator. Do not prepare more than 2 hours in advance of serving.

For the whipped cream, beat the whipping cream in a mixing bowl until soft peaks form. Add the sugar and vanilla and mix well.

To serve, cut the shortcakes horizontally into halves. Arrange 1 bottom half on each of 8 dessert plates. Top each with some of the berry mixture and a dollop of whipped cream. Top with the remaining shortbread halves. Serve immediately. A preheated oven is recommended.

BUTTERMILK PIE

MAKES 2 PIES

1 cup (2 sticks) butter, melted and cooled
6 eggs, beaten
2 1/2 cups sugar
1/2 cup flour
1 teaspoon salt
1 cup buttermilk
1 teaspoon vanilla extract
2 unbaked (9-inch) pie shells

Blend the butter and eggs in a bowl. Add a mixture of the sugar, flour, salt, buttermilk and vanilla and mix well. Spoon half the buttermilk filling into each pie shell. Bake at 350 degrees for 45 minutes. Remove to a wire rack to cool.

CHESS PIE

SERVES 6 TO 8

1 1/4 cups sugar
1/2 cup (1 stick) butter, softened
1 tablespoon flour
2 eggs
1/4 cup half-and-half
1 teaspoon vanilla extract
1 unbaked (9-inch) pie shell

Beat the sugar, butter and flour in a mixing bowl until creamy. Beat in the eggs 1 at a time. Add the half-and-half and vanilla and beat until blended. Spoon into the pie shell. Bake at 350 degrees for 40 to 45 minutes or until set. Remove to a wire rack to cool.

SOUTHERN PECAN PIE

SERVES 8

1 cup light corn syrup
1 cup sugar
2 eggs, beaten
2 tablespoons butter or margarine, melted
1 teaspoon vanilla extract
1/8 teaspoon salt
1 cup pecans
1 unbaked (10-inch) deep-dish pie shell

Mix the first 6 ingredients in a bowl. Stir in the pecans. Spoon the pecan mixture into the pie shell. Bake at 400 degrees for 15 minutes; reduce the oven temperature to 350 degrees. Bake for 30 to 35 minutes longer or until set. Remove to a wire rack to cool.

FUDGE PIE

SERVES 6 TO 8

1 cup sugar
1/4 cup each baking cocoa and flour
1/2 cup (1 stick) butter, melted
2 eggs, lightly beaten
1 teaspoon vanilla extract
1 unbaked (9-inch) pie shell

Combine the sugar, baking cocoa and flour in a bowl and mix well. Stir in the butter. Add the eggs and vanilla and mix well. Spoon the chocolate filling into the pie shell. Bake at 325 degrees for 30 minutes or until the center is set. Remove to a wire rack to cool.

IRON SKILLET CHOCOLATE PIE
SERVES 6 TO 8

CHOCOLATE PIE

2 tablespoons (rounded) butter
1 cup sugar
2 tablespoons (heaping) flour
2 tablespoons baking cocoa
1 cup milk
2 egg yolks
1 teaspoon vanilla extract
1 baked (9-inch) pie shell

MERINGUE

2 egg whites
1/4 cup sugar

For the pie, heat the butter in a cast-iron skillet over low heat. Stir in a mixture of the sugar, flour and baking cocoa. Whisk the milk and egg yolks in a bowl until blended. Add the milk mixture to the baking cocoa mixture and mix well. Cook until thickened, stirring constantly. Stir in the vanilla. Spoon the chocolate filling into the pie shell.

For the meringue, beat the egg whites in a mixing bowl until soft peaks form. Add the sugar gradually, beating constantly until stiff but not dry peaks form. Spread the meringue over the top of the pie, sealing to the edge. Bake at 325 degrees just until brown. Remove to a wire rack to cool. A preheated oven is recommended.

COCONUT CREAM PIE
SERVES 6 TO 8

1 cup sugar
3 egg yolks
1 teaspoon vanilla extract
1/8 teaspoon salt
2 cups milk
6 tablespoons flour
1/2 cup flaked coconut
1 baked (9-inch) pie shell
3 egg whites
2 tablespoons sugar
1/2 cup flaked coconut

Combine 1 cup sugar, egg yolks, vanilla and salt in a double boiler and mix well. Add the milk and flour alternately, mixing well after each addition. Cook until thickened, stirring constantly. Remove from the heat. Stir in 1/2 cup coconut. Spoon the coconut mixture into the pie shell.

Beat the egg whites in a mixing bowl until soft peaks form. Add 2 tablespoons sugar gradually, beating constantly until stiff but not dry peaks form. Spread the meringue over the pie, sealing to the edge. Sprinkle with 1/2 cup coconut. Bake at 350 degrees until golden brown. Remove to a wire rack to cool. A preheated oven is recommended.

APPLE DUMPLING CRESCENTS

SERVES 8

1 cup sugar
1 cup orange juice
1/2 cup (1 stick) butter
1 teaspoon vanilla extract
1 (8-count) can crescent rolls
4 McIntosh apples, peeled and
cut into halves
cinnamon to taste

Combine the sugar, orange juice and butter in a saucepan. Bring to a boil, stirring occasionally. Remove from the heat. Stir in the vanilla. Unroll the crescent roll dough and separate into 8 triangles.

Roll 1 triangle on a hard surface and wrap around 1 apple half. Arrange seam side down in a baking dish. Repeat the process with the remaining triangles and apple halves. Sprinkle with cinnamon and drizzle the orange juice mixture over the top. Sprinkle with cinnamon again if desired. Bake at 350 degrees for 30 minutes. Serve hot with ice cream. A preheated oven is recommended.

FRUIT COBBLER

SERVES 4 TO 6

2 cups blackberries, raspberries, blueberries
or chopped peaches
3/4 cup sugar
1/2 cup (1 stick) butter
3/4 cup flour
1 cup sugar
2 teaspoons baking powder
3/4 cup buttermilk

Toss the fruit and 3/4 cup sugar in a bowl. Melt the butter in a shallow baking dish. Mix the flour, 1 cup sugar and baking powder in a bowl. Stir in the buttermilk. Spoon the flour mixture into the prepared baking dish and top with the fruit mixture; do not stir. Bake at 300 degrees for 1 hour. A preheated oven is recommended.

MAGGIE'S
ICE CREAM DELIGHTS
S E R V E S 6 T O 8

1/2 gallon vanilla bean ice cream, softened
1 cup amaretto, or liqueur of choice
whipped cream to taste
cinnamon to taste

Combine the ice cream and liqueur in a bowl and mix well. Spoon the mixture into serving cups. Freeze until firm. Top each serving with whipped cream and sprinkle with cinnamon.

CANTALOUPE SORBET
S E R V E S 4 T O 6

1 cup sugar
1 cup water
1 ripe cantaloupe, chopped
juice of 1 lime
4 to 6 lime slices

Combine the sugar and water in a saucepan and mix well. Cook until the sugar dissolves, stirring frequently. Continue cooking for a few minutes longer, stirring occasionally. Let stand until cool.

Process the cantaloupe in batches in a food processor until puréed. Combine the puréed cantaloupe, sugar syrup and lime juice in a glass bowl and mix well. Freeze, covered, until firm. Spoon the sorbet into dessert bowls and garnish each serving with a lime slice.

The Polks entertained on a rather lavish scale. They hosted dinner guests up to three times per week. Large quantities of food and wine were purchased through a number of local markets. A surviving grocery account book gives a glimpse into dining at the Polk White House. Just in the month of August of 1846, they consumed 115 lbs. of beef, 10 whole chickens, 102 lbs. of corned beef, 80 lbs. of veal, 134 lbs. of ham, 19 dozen eggs, and much more. Fish of various kinds was also regular fare, along with the unusual courses of robin, snipe, and calves' heads.

COFFEE-TOFFEE MERINGUE DELIGHT

SERVES 12

MERINGUE

vegetable oil

1/2 cup egg whites, at room temperature

1/8 teaspoon salt

1/8 teaspoon cream of tartar

1 cup sugar

1 teaspoon vanilla extract

1 teaspoon white vinegar

FILLING

1/2 gallon coffee ice cream, softened

12 (1.4-ounce) chocolate toffee candy bars, crushed

2 cups whipping cream

For the meringue, chill a clean dry bowl in the freezer. Line a baking sheet with foil and brush the foil lightly with oil. Beat the egg whites, salt and cream of tartar in the chilled bowl until foamy. Add 1/2 cup of the sugar 1 tablespoon at a time, beating 30 to 45 seconds after each addition. Beat in the vanilla and vinegar. Add the remaining 1/2 cup sugar 1 tablespoon at a time, beating 30 to 45 seconds after each addition. Continue beating for 2 minutes longer.

Shape the meringue into a 9-inch ring on the prepared baking sheet or into individual meringue shells. Bake at 200 degrees for 1 1/2 hours. Turn off the oven; do not open the door. Let the meringue stand with the door closed for 6 to 10 hours. Store in an airtight container for up to 2 days or freeze for future use. Do not make meringues on humid or rainy days.

For the filling, combine the ice cream with half the crushed candy in a bowl and mix well; refreeze. Scoop the ice cream mixture into balls and freeze in muffin cups.

Beat the whipping cream in a mixing bowl until soft peaks form. Fold in 3/4 of the remaining crushed candy.

To serve, fill the meringue ring with the ice cream balls. Frost with the whipped cream mixture and sprinkle with the remaining crushed candy. Serve immediately. A preheated oven is recommended.

GRAND MARNIER FROZEN SOUFFLÉ

S E R V E S   8   T O   1 0

1 cup sugar
1/3 cup water
2 tablespoons grated orange zest
6 egg yolks
1/4 cup Grand Marnier
2 cups whipping cream
1 (3-ounce) package frozen ladyfingers

Fit a 4-cup soufflé dish with a greased 6-inch strip of double thickness waxed paper to form a collar, extending 2 inches above the rim. Tie with kitchen twine to secure. Bring the sugar, water and orange zest to a boil in a saucepan over medium heat. Boil until a candy thermometer registers 225 degrees. Beat the egg yolks in a mixing bowl until thick and pale yellow. Add the sugar syrup to the egg yolks gradually, beating constantly until thickened. Let stand until cool. Beat in the liqueur.

Beat the whipping cream in a mixing bowl until soft peaks form. Fold the whipped cream into the liqueur mixture. Spoon enough of the custard into the prepared dish to measure 2 inches. Top with half the ladyfingers. Layer with half the remaining custard and the remaining ladyfingers. Top with the remaining custard. Freeze, covered, for 6 hours. Serve with additional whipped cream flavored with additional Grand Marnier. Garnish with fresh berries or meringue mushrooms, or as desired.

A congressional family's life in Washington was not an easy one. Spending three months in rented rooms, then leaving for home, not always knowing if one would return, meant many sad goodbyes to friends and housemates. Sarah Polk received many warm expressions of friendship. Supreme Court Justice Joseph Story, a Whig in politics, but an admirer of Sarah Polk, saw fit to write her a farewell poem. His warm wishes concluded with the lines:

"Farewell; and when thy
distant home
cheered by thy smile shall be
To know the past thick
fancies come,
I ask one thought of me."

FRENCH BREAD PUDDING WITH BOURBON SAUCE

SERVES 8 TO 10

BREAD PUDDING

1 cup sugar
1/2 cup (1 stick) butter, softened
2 cups heavy cream
5 eggs, beaten
1/4 teaspoon cinnamon

1 tablespoon vanilla extract
1/2 cup raisins
12 (1-inch-thick) slices French bread, crusts removed

BOURBON SAUCE

1 cup sugar
1 cup heavy cream
1 tablespoon butter
1/4 teaspoon cinnamon

1/4 cup water
1/2 teaspoon cornstarch
1 tablespoon bourbon

For the pudding, beat the sugar and butter in a mixing bowl until creamy. Add the heavy cream, eggs, cinnamon, vanilla and raisins and mix well. Spoon into a 9×9-inch baking pan, 1³/4 inches deep. Arrange the bread slices in a single layer over the egg mixture, pressing lightly to ensure total coverage. Let stand for 5 minutes. Turn the bread slices and press lightly to ensure coverage. Let stand for 10 minutes.

Place the baking pan in a larger baking pan. Add enough water to the larger baking pan to reach halfway up the sides of the smaller pan. Bake, covered, at 350 degrees for 35 to 40 minutes; remove the cover. Bake for 10 minutes longer. The custard will be soft.

For the sauce, combine the sugar, heavy cream, butter and cinnamon in a saucepan. Bring to a boil, stirring occasionally. Mix the water and cornstarch in a small bowl. Add the cornstarch mixture to the cream mixture and mix well. Cook until the sauce is thickened and clear, stirring frequently. Remove from the heat. Stir in the bourbon.

To serve, spoon the warm pudding onto dessert plates or into dessert goblets and drizzle with the warm sauce. Serve immediately. A preheated oven is recommended.

BANANA PUDDING

S E R V E S   6   T O   8

1 1/2 cups sugar
3 tablespoons flour
3 egg yolks, beaten
3 cups milk
3 tablespoons butter
1 teaspoon vanilla extract
1 (12- to 16-ounce) package vanilla wafers
5 ripe bananas, sliced
3 egg whites
1/3 cup sugar

Mix 1 1/2 cups sugar and flour in a saucepan. Stir in the egg yolks. Add the milk gradually, stirring constantly. Cook over medium heat until thickened, stirring constantly. Remove from the heat. Stir in the butter and vanilla.

Alternate layers of the vanilla wafers, bananas and custard in an ovenproof baking dish until all of the ingredients are used, ending with the custard. Beat the egg whites in a mixing bowl until foamy. Add 1/3 cup sugar gradually, beating constantly until stiff but not dry peaks form. Spread the meringue over the top of the prepared layers, sealing to the edge. Bake at 350 degrees until light brown. A preheated oven is recommended.

Sarah Polk was presented with gifts from admirers from home and abroad. The Polks refused gifts of great value, but they did accept small presents. Authors often sent Mrs. Polk their books. She made it her habit to read as many as possible so that upon meeting the authors, she would be able to converse intelligently about their work. Other gifts included an ornate inkwell made from the volcanic ash from Mt. Vesuvius, a bonnet made of "140,000 yards" of glass, costume gifts given by Native American tribes, and a large portrait of Hernando Cortez that was brought back after the Mexican-American War.

FIESTA FLAN
SERVES 6 TO 8

1 cup sugar   *1/8 teaspoon salt*
4 cups milk   *4 eggs*
1/2 cup sugar   *6 egg yolks*
1 (2-inch) cinnamon stick

Sprinkle 1 cup sugar in a heavy saucepan. Heat over medium heat until the sugar melts and turns caramel colored, stirring constantly with a wooden spoon. Pour the caramelized sugar into a 1 1/2-quart mold and tilt the mold to ensure even coverage over the bottom and side. Work quickly as the caramel hardens fast.

Combine the milk, 1/2 cup sugar, cinnamon stick and salt in a 2- to 3-quart saucepan. Bring to a brisk simmer, stirring occasionally. Simmer for 15 minutes or until the milk is reduced by 1/2 cup, stirring occasionally. Let stand until cool.

Beat the eggs and egg yolks in a mixing bowl until blended. Add the eggs to the milk mixture and mix well. Strain the milk mixture into the prepared mold, discarding the solids. Set the mold in a baking pan. Add enough warm water to the baking pan to reach 1 inch up the side of the mold. Bake at 350 degrees for 50 to 60 minutes or until a knife inserted in the center comes out clean. Remove the mold from the baking pan. Let stand until cool. Chill, covered, in the refrigerator.

To serve, run a sharp knife around the edge of the mold and invert the flan onto a serving platter with sides, allowing the caramel to drizzle down the side of the flan. Cut into wedges. A preheated oven is recommended.

MACAROON PUDDING

SERVES 8 TO 10

1¹/2 envelopes unflavored gelatin
¹/2 cup water
2 cups milk
1 cup sugar
3 egg yolks
18 macaroons, crumbled
3 egg whites, stiffly beaten
1 teaspoon vanilla extract
whipped cream
maraschino cherries

Dissolve the gelatin in the water in a small bowl and mix well. Heat the milk in a double boiler, stirring constantly. Whisk the sugar and eggs yolks in a bowl until blended. Pour the warm milk over the egg yolk mixture. Return the mixture to the double boiler. Stir in the gelatin mixture.

Cook until the mixture coats a spoon, stirring frequently. Remove from the heat. Fold the macaroons, egg whites and vanilla into the gelatin mixture. Spoon into a greased 2-quart mold. Chill, covered, for 2 to 10 hours or until set. Garnish each serving with whipped cream and maraschino cherries.

Despite Sarah Polk's Scotch-Irish ancestry and her Tennessee frontier upbringing, Washington society dubbed her "the Spanish Donna." This unexpected nickname was purportedly coined by a visiting Englishwoman who commented that Sarah's "hair is very black, and her dark eyes and complexion remind one of a Spanish donna." The description also reflected the First Lady's fondness for elegant lace fans and stylish headdresses, as well as her interest in European fashion and decorative arts. For many Washingtonians, Sarah's keen intelligence and political acumen seemed as exotic and appealing as her striking appearance.

KILLER HOT FUDGE SAUCE

MAKES 2 CUPS

1/2 cup (1 stick) butter
4 ounces unsweetened chocolate
1 (14-ounce) can sweetened condensed milk
6 tablespoons evaporated milk
1/8 teaspoon salt
sugar to taste

---

*H*eat the butter and chocolate in a heavy saucepan over medium heat until blended, stirring frequently. Stir in the condensed milk and evaporated milk. Cook until blended, stirring frequently. Remove from the heat. Stir in the salt and sugar. Use immediately, or store, covered, in the refrigerator. Reheat as needed in the microwave, or over low heat in a saucepan. Drizzle the sauce over ice cream, cake or fresh fruits.

ZESTY LEMON SAUCE

VARIABLE

2/3 cup sugar
zest of 1 lemon
5 egg yolks
1/2 cup lemon juice
1/8 teaspoon salt
1/2 cup (1 stick) butter

---

*P*rocess the sugar and lemon zest in a food processor until the lemon zest is minced. Add the egg yolks, lemon juice and salt. Process until mixed. Heat the butter in a saucepan until melted. Add the hot butter to the lemon mixture, processing constantly until blended. Pour the lemon mixture into a saucepan. Cook over low heat until thickened, stirring constantly; do not boil. Store, covered, in the refrigerator. Serve over pound cake or spoon into tart shells.

MICROWAVE MAGIC TOFFEE

MAKES 1 POUND

1/2 cup finely chopped pecans or almonds
1/2 cup (1 stick) margarine (do not use butter)
1 cup sugar
1/4 cup water
1 teaspoon salt
3/4 cup semisweet chocolate morsels
1/4 cup finely chopped pecans or almonds

Sprinkle 1/2 cup pecans in a 9-inch circle on a greased baking sheet. Coat the top 2 inches of a 2 1/2-quart microwave-safe glass bowl with some of the margarine and place the remaining margarine in the bowl. Add the sugar, water and salt to the bowl; do not stir.

Microwave on High for 11 minutes or just until the mixture begins to turn light brown. Pour over the pecans. Sprinkle with the chocolate morsels. Let stand for 1 minute. Spread the chocolate over the pecan mixture and sprinkle with 1/4 cup pecans. Chill until firm. Break into bite-size pieces.

During James K. Polk's years as a U.S. congressman, his wife enjoyed discussing politics with other legislators. These politicians were startled and amused when Sarah openly disagreed with her husband on issues such as paper currency. James K. Polk questioned the reliability of paper bank notes and advocated the use of only gold and silver coins as currency. On one occasion, Sarah slyly reprimanded her spouse and his Democratic colleagues by declaring, "You and your friends certainly are mistaken about that bank question. Why, if we use gold and silver all the time, a lady can scarcely carry enough money with her."

DEEP SOUTH PRALINES

MAKES 2 DOZEN

2 cups sugar
1 teaspoon baking soda
1/8 teaspoon salt
1 cup buttermilk
2 1/3 cups pecans
2 tablespoons butter

Combine the sugar, baking soda and salt in a heavy saucepan and mix well. Stir in the buttermilk. Bring to a boil, stirring constantly. Boil for 5 minutes or until a candy thermometer registers 210 degrees, stirring constantly. Stir in the pecans and butter. Return to a boil.

Boil for 5 minutes or until a candy thermometer registers 230 degrees, soft-ball stage. Remove from the heat and cool slightly. Beat until thickened and creamy. Immediately drop by tablespoonfuls onto waxed paper. Let stand until firm. Store in an airtight container.

PUDGY FUDGE

MAKES 108

3 cups sugar
3/4 cup (1 1/2 sticks) margarine
2/3 cup evaporated milk
2 cups (12 ounces) semisweet chocolate chips
1 (7-ounce) jar marshmallow creme
1 cup chopped pecans
1 teaspoon vanilla extract

Mix the first 3 ingredients in a heavy 3-quart saucepan. Bring to a rolling boil over medium heat, stirring constantly. Boil for 5 minutes or until a candy thermometer registers 235 degrees, stirring constantly. Remove from the heat.

Add the chocolate chips to the hot mixture and mix well. Stir in the marshmallow creme, pecans and vanilla. Beat until mixed. Spoon into a buttered 9×13-inch dish. Let stand until cool.

ANGEL FOOD SQUARES

VARIABLE

1 (1-pound) package confectioners' sugar
1 cup (2 sticks) butter, softened
2 tablespoons light rum
1 egg white
1 angel food cake, cut into squares
2 cups finely chopped pecans

Beat the first 4 ingredients in a mixing bowl. Spread the mixture over the surfaces of the cake squares and roll each square in the pecans.

APRICOT BARS

MAKES 2 DOZEN

1/2 cup (1 stick) butter
1/4 cup sugar
1 1/2 cups flour
2 egg yolks
1/2 teaspoon salt
3 tablespoons apricot jam
2 egg whites
1/2 cup sugar
1 teaspoon vanilla extract
1/4 cup coarsely ground walnuts

Beat the butter and 1/4 cup sugar in a mixing bowl until creamy. Add the flour, egg yolks and salt. Beat until blended, scraping the bowl occasionally. Spoon the batter into a greased 8×8-inch baking pan. Bake at 350 degrees for 10 minutes. Spread with the jam.

Beat the egg whites in a mixing bowl until soft peaks form. Add 1/2 cup sugar and vanilla gradually, beating constantly until stiff but not dry peaks form. Spread the meringue over the baked layer and sprinkle with the walnuts. Bake for 20 to 30 minutes longer or until golden brown. Cool in the pan on a wire rack. Cut into squares. You may substitute raspberry jam or plum jam for the apricot jam. A preheated oven is recommended.

James and Sarah Polk were the first First Family to be widely photographed. During their administration, the first exterior and interior images of the White House were taken. A daguerreotype of President Polk and his Cabinet is the first of its kind. Yet another remarkable image taken at that time shows two Presidents and three First Ladies. The venerable fourth First Lady, Dolley Madison, stands near President and Mrs. Polk, while Secretary of State and future President James Buchanan, along with his niece Harriet Lane, who would act as his official White House hostess, complete the group.

RASPBERRY CHEESECAKE BROWNIES

MAKES 3 TO 4 DOZEN

BROWNIES

4 ounces semisweet chocolate
2 ounces unsweetened chocolate
1/2 cup (1 stick) butter
1 1/4 cups sugar
3 eggs

3/4 cup flour
1 1/2 teaspoons vanilla extract
3/4 teaspoon salt
1 cup seedless raspberry jam
1 tablespoon lemon juice

CREAM CHEESE TOPPING

8 ounces cream cheese, softened
2/3 cup sugar
1 egg
2 teaspoons fresh lemon juice
1/2 teaspoon vanilla extract

1/4 teaspoon salt
2 tablespoons flour
1 1/2 cups fresh or frozen raspberries
1 tablespoon sugar

For the brownies, heat the semisweet chocolate, unsweetened chocolate and butter in a double boiler over hot water until blended, stirring frequently. Remove from the heat. Let stand until cool. Whisk in the sugar until blended. Add the eggs 1 at a time, whisking after each addition until smooth. Whisk in the flour, vanilla and salt until blended. Spread the batter in a buttered and floured 9×13-inch baking pan. Heat the jam and lemon juice in a saucepan until melted, stirring frequently. Spread the jam mixture over the prepared layer.

For the topping, beat the cream cheese and 2/3 cup sugar in a mixing bowl until light and fluffy. Beat in the egg, lemon juice, vanilla and salt. Add the flour and beat until smooth. Spread the cream cheese mixture over the prepared layers. Sprinkle with the raspberries and 1 tablespoon sugar. Bake at 350 degrees for 35 to 40 minutes or until light brown; do not overbake. Cool in the pan on a wire rack. Chill, covered, for 6 to 8 hours. Cut into squares. A preheated oven is recommended.

CAREY'S BROWNIES

MAKES 4 DOZEN

4 ounces unsweetened chocolate
2 cups sugar
1 cup (2 sticks) margarine
4 eggs
1 cup sifted flour
2 teaspoons vanilla extract
1 cup chopped walnuts or pecans

Heat the chocolate in a double boiler over hot water until melted. Remove from the heat. Beat the sugar and margarine in a mixing bowl until creamy. Add the eggs and beat until blended. Beat in the chocolate, flour and vanilla. Stir in the walnuts. Spoon the batter into a greased 9×13-inch baking pan. Bake at 325 degrees for 35 minutes. Cool in the pan on a wire rack. Cut as desired. Store in an airtight container. A preheated oven is recommended.

DUCK RIVER MUD

MAKES 4 DOZEN

1 recipe Carey's Brownies
1 (16-ounce) package miniature marshmallows
1/2 cup (1 stick) butter
1 1/2 cups sugar
1 tablespoon (heaping) baking cocoa
1/3 teaspoon salt
1/4 cup milk
1/4 cup light corn syrup
1 teaspoon vanilla extract

Prepare and bake the brownies. Remove the brownies from the oven and immediately sprinkle with the marshmallows. Let stand, covered with foil, until the marshmallows melt.

Place the butter in the freezer. Combine the sugar, baking cocoa and salt in a heavy 2-quart saucepan and mix well. Mix the milk and corn syrup in a bowl. Stir the milk mixture into the baking cocoa mixture; cover. Bring to a boil. Boil for 3 minutes. Remove from the heat and add the butter. Beat with a hand mixer until thickened. Stir in the vanilla. Pour the chocolate mixture over the marshmallows. Let stand until cool. Cut as desired. Store in an airtight container. A preheated oven is recommended.

BEST-EVER CHOCOLATE CHIP COOKIES

MAKES 2 DOZEN

4 cups flour
1 1/2 teaspoons baking soda
1/2 teaspoon salt
1 cup (2 sticks) unsalted butter, cut into
1-ounce slices
2 cups packed dark brown sugar
2 eggs
2 tablespoons dark rum
1 teaspoon vanilla extract
4 cups (24 ounces) semisweet chocolate chips

Sift the flour, baking soda and salt onto a sheet of waxed paper. Beat the unsalted butter and brown sugar in a mixing bowl for 4 minutes or until creamy, scraping the bowl occasionally. Add the eggs, rum and vanilla. Beat at medium speed for 1 minute. Add the dry ingredients and beat at low speed for 1 minute. Add the chocolate chips. Beat at low speed for 30 seconds.

Place 2 heaping tablespoons of the dough for each cookie on each of 4 nonstick cookie sheets, allowing 6 evenly spaced cookies per cookie sheet. Place the cookie sheets on the top and center oven racks. Bake at 300 degrees for 14 to 15 minutes. Rotate the baking sheets from the top to the center racks and rotate each 180 degrees. Bake for 14 to 15 minutes longer. Cool on the cookie sheets for 30 minutes. Store in an airtight container. For a soft-baked cookie, bake at 325 degrees for 20 minutes. A preheated oven is recommended.

MOCHA CHIP COOKIES

MAKES 2 DOZEN

2 tablespoons instant coffee powder
2 tablespoons boiling water
1 1/4 cups flour
3/4 teaspoon baking soda
1/2 teaspoon salt
1/2 cup (1 stick) butter
1/2 cup sugar
1/2 cup packed light brown sugar
1 egg
1/2 cup (3 ounces) semisweet chocolate chips,
melted and cooled
1 1/2 cups (9 ounces) semisweet
chocolate chips
1 cup chopped walnuts

Dissolve the coffee powder in the boiling water in a heatproof bowl. Let stand until cool. Mix the flour, baking soda and salt together. Beat the butter, sugar and brown sugar in a mixing bowl until creamy, scraping the bowl occasionally. Beat in the coffee. Add the egg and melted chocolate chips and beat until smooth. Stir in the dry ingredients, 1 1/2 cups chocolate chips and walnuts.

Drop by tablespoonfuls onto a cookie sheet. Bake at 350 degrees for 10 to 12 minutes or until crisp around the edges. Cool on the cookie sheet for 2 to 3 minutes. Remove to a wire rack to cool completely. Store in an airtight container. A preheated oven is recommended.

MILLIONAIRES

MAKES 4 DOZEN

SHORTBREAD CRUST

2 cups flour
1/2 teaspoon salt
2/3 cup butter, softened
1/2 cup sugar

TOFFEE FILLING AND ICING

1/2 cup (1 stick) butter
1/2 cup sweetened condensed milk
2 tablespoons light corn syrup
1 teaspoon vanilla extract
1 1/2 cups (9 ounces) semisweet chocolate chips, melted

For the crust, sift the flour and salt together. Process the butter and sugar in a food processor until creamy. Add the flour mixture and process until grainy. Press over the bottom of a greased 9×12-inch baking pan. Bake at 350 degrees for 20 to 30 minutes or until light brown. Let stand until cool.

For the filling, combine the butter, condensed milk, corn syrup and vanilla in a saucepan. Bring to a boil, whisking occasionally. Boil for 4 minutes, whisking occasionally. Cool slightly. Spread the filling over the baked layer. Let stand until cool. Spread the melted chocolate over the prepared layers. Let stand until set. Cut into squares. Store in an airtight container. A preheated oven is recommended.

As a political wife, Sarah Polk had opportunities to travel throughout the country. During James K. Polk's years as a congressman in Washington, D.C., he and Sarah returned to Tennessee every summer by a different route. They traveled by coach through the Virginia mountains, by steamer on the Ohio River, and even by canal boat on the Erie Canal on a circuitous journey that included Niagara Falls. Sarah enjoyed the trips despite the hazards of early-19th-century travel. She had to be rescued from an overturned stagecoach in Virginia and from a coach caught in the current of a swollen Tennessee stream.

BUTTER PECAN COOKIES

MAKES 3 DOZEN

1 (2-layer) package butter pecan cake mix
1/2 cup (1 stick) butter, melted
2 eggs
1 teaspoon vanilla extract
1 (7-ounce) package almond brickle chips
1/2 cup chopped pecans

*B*eat the cake mix, butter, eggs and vanilla in a mixing bowl until blended. Stir in the brickle chips and pecans.

Drop by spoonfuls 2 inches apart onto a greased cookie sheet. Bake at 350 degrees for 8 minutes. Cool on the cookie sheet for 2 minutes. Remove to a wire rack to cool completely. Store in an airtight container. A preheated oven is recommended.

OATMEAL CHERRY CHIP COOKIES

MAKES 2 DOZEN

1 cup flour
1/2 teaspoon baking soda
1/4 teaspoon salt
1/2 cup (1 stick) plus 2 tablespoons unsalted butter
1/2 cup sugar
1/2 cup packed dark brown sugar
1 egg
1 teaspoon vanilla extract
1/2 teaspoon almond extract
1 cup old-fashioned oats
1 1/2 cups (9 ounces) semisweet chocolate chips
1 cup dried tart cherries or craisins
1/2 cup slivered almonds, toasted

*S*ift the flour, baking soda and salt together. Beat the unsalted butter, sugar and brown sugar in a mixing bowl until creamy. Add the egg and flavorings and beat until blended. Beat in the dry ingredients until smooth. Stir in the oats, chocolate chips, cherries and almonds.

Drop by rounded tablespoonfuls 2 inches apart onto a cookie sheet lined with baking parchment. Bake at 325 degrees for 15 to 18 minutes or until light brown. Cool on the cookie sheet for 2 minutes. Remove to a wire rack to cool completely. Store in an airtight container. A preheated oven is recommended.

MAURY MOLASSES COOKIES

MAKES 2 DOZEN

2 cups flour
2 teaspoons baking soda
1/2 teaspoon ground cloves
1/2 teaspoon cinnamon
1/2 teaspoon salt
1/2 teaspoon ginger
3/4 cup shortening, melted and cooled
1 cup sugar
1/4 cup molasses
1 egg
1/4 cup sugar

Sift the flour, baking soda, cloves, cinnamon, salt and ginger into a bowl and mix well. Combine the shortening, 1 cup sugar, molasses and egg in a mixing bowl. Beat until creamy. Add the flour mixture and beat until blended. Chill, covered, for 1 to 10 hours (the colder the better).

Shape the dough into 1-inch balls and roll in 1/4 cup sugar. Arrange the balls 2 inches apart on a cookie sheet. Bake at 375 degrees for 8 to 10 minutes or until light brown; do not overbake. Cool on the cookie sheet for 2 minutes. Remove to a wire rack to cool completely. The cookies will appear partially cooked and cracked. A preheated oven is recommended.

Although Sarah Polk supported her husband's political ambitions and admired his dedication, she worried constantly that his hard work was ruining his health. During James K. Polk's difficult (and ultimately unsuccessful) campaign for reelection as Tennessee's governor in 1841, Sarah sent him a letter saying, "When I think of the labour and fatigue you have to undergo, I feel sad and melancholy, and conclude that success is not worth the labour." She repeated her concern in a later letter: "Let the result be what it may, so you do not destroy your health or kill yourself with fatigue."

Super Sugar Cookies
M A K E S   3   D O Z E N

Cookies

3 cups flour	1 teaspoon vanilla extract
2 teaspoons cream of tartar	1 cup (2 sticks) margarine
1 teaspoon baking soda	1 cup sugar
2 tablespoons milk	1 egg

Confectioners' Sugar Icing

3 cups confectioners' sugar	1 to 2 tablespoons cream
1/2 cup (1 stick) butter, softened	1 teaspoon vanilla extract
1 egg (optional)	food coloring (optional)

For the cookies, mix the flour, cream of tartar and baking soda together. Mix the milk and vanilla in a small bowl. Beat the margarine and sugar in a mixing bowl until creamy. Add the egg and beat until blended. Add the milk mixture alternately with the flour mixture, beating well after each addition. Chill, covered, in the refrigerator.

Roll the dough very thin on a lightly floured surface. Cut with your favorite cookie cutter. Arrange the cookies 2 inches apart on a cookie sheet. Bake at 325 degrees for 8 to 10 minutes or until light brown. Cool on the cookie sheet for 2 minutes. Remove to a wire rack to cool completely.

For the icing, combine the confectioners' sugar, butter, egg, cream and vanilla in a mixing bowl. Beat until smooth and to a spreading consistency, scraping the bowl occasionally. Tint with food coloring if desired. Spread the icing over the tops of the cooled cookies. To avoid raw eggs that may carry salmonella, we suggest using an equivalent amount of pasteurized egg substitute. A preheated oven is recommended.

SURPRISE COOKIES

MAKES 5 DOZEN

1 cup (2 sticks) butter
$1/2$ cup sugar
$1^1/2$ cups plus 1 tablespoon flour
$1/2$ teaspoon vanilla extract
$3/4$ cup coarsely crumbled potato chips
confectioners' sugar to taste

*B*eat the butter and sugar in a mixing bowl until creamy, scraping the bowl occasionally. Add the flour and vanilla gradually, beating constantly until blended. Fold in the potato chips. Drop by rounded teaspoonfuls 2 inches apart onto an ungreased cookie sheet. Flatten the cookies gently with a moistened fork.

Bake at 300 degrees for 15 to 20 minutes or until light brown. Cool on the cookie sheet for 2 minutes. Remove to a wire rack to cool completely. Sift confectioners' sugar over the tops of the cookies. Store in an airtight container. A preheated oven is recommended.

*W*hen news of James K. Polk's election to the Presidency reached Columbia, Tennessee, excited townspeople gathered at the Polks' cottage to offer congratulations. Several gentlemen tried to control the rush of people and told Mrs. Polk, "We will not let the crowd in, because the street is muddy, and your carpets and furniture will be spoiled." True to her husband's democratic sentiments, Sarah replied, "The house is thrown open to everybody. Let them all come in; they will not hurt the carpets." Sarah later confirmed that the well-wishers had "left no marks except the marks of respect."

COOKBOOK COMMITTEE

Jody Ball
Lisa Butler
Kay Curtis
Sandy Finney

Lonsdale Green
Deb Hartman
Rachel Hughes
Kadi Lehnhart

Emily McKnight
Nancy Hickman McNulty
Roben Mounger

A SPECIAL THANKS TO

Virginia Alexander
Alice Algood
Ernie Allen
Betsy Anderson
Jane Locke Anderson
Janelle Arnold
Shelly Ayers
Sara Babb
Jody Ball
Katherine Barnes
Betsy Barr
Marjorie Barr
Jennifer Barrier
Elizabeth and Billy Blackstone
Diane Bolton
Melinda Britt
Lee R. Brown
Aylene Buchanan
Lisa Butler
Martha Sue Cain
Bonnie Callawaert
Kitty Chaffin
Surama Choksi
Lucinda Cockrell
Vanessa and John Colley
Eunice Colmore
Griffie Cook
Rose Cook
Gloria Cox
Betty Crabtree
Eva James Crichton

Bitty Crozier
Jane Cunningham
Kay Curtis
Leta Cutler
Gloria Dale
Mary Dale
Annie Daniel
Sandra-Kay Daniels
Tara Daniels
Jordan Delcambre
Susan Dell
Katie DeWeese
Betsy Duling
Sue Dunnebacke
Gayle Eadie
Sue Edwards
Jean Evans
Barbara Finney
Sandy and John Finney
Carolyn Fisher
Sheila Fleming
Mary Jo Folger
Lyllian Ford
Chloe Fort
Marie Frakes
Dot Frierson
Netta Fry
Amy Gentry
Gail Gilliam
Maribeth Gordon
Robyn Graham

Lonsdale and Kelly Green
Pebble Rainey Hager
Polly Ann Halliday
Sandy Halliday
Connie Hardin
Jennie Jo Hardison
Carolina Harlan
Ginger Harlan
Jean Harlan
Jennie Harlan
Peggy Harmon
Deb Hartman
Lisa Van Harwell
Van Harwell
Helen Hays
Cindy Hedrick
Margaret Hewgley
Sarah High
Mark Hines
Roxanne Howell
Rachel Hughes
Claudia Jack
Kim Jameson
Sarah Johnson
Jim Jones
Martha Jones
Tiny Jones
Bridget Jones Kelley
Martha H. Kelley
Betty and Sam Kennedy
Glenda Kennedy

Mary Susan Kennedy
Lucy Scott Kuykendall
Anne Lacey Lawrence
Kadi Lehnhart
Beth Lindsey
Kay Lindsey
Anne C. Lineberger
Jean Locke
Wilma Locke
Cornelia Lovell
Susan Lovell
Tom Lucas
Marjanne Lunde
Sarah Maddux
Perre Coleman Magness
Perre Magness
Lucy Malone
Kristi Martin
Cleo Mayfield
Joyce Mays
Lucie Mays
Sydney McClain
Bill McEwen
Emily McKnight
Louise McKnight
Ann Marie McNamara
Nancy Hickman McNulty
Virginia Meece
Mary Jane Miles
Deborah Molder
Dawn and Edward Moore
Edie Moore
Gale Courtney Moore
Jane Moore
Linda Moore
Nancy Moore
Mary Lou Morton
Roben and Dalton Mounger

Sherri Naddy
Elizabeth Nesbitt
Maggie and John Olson
Lois Orr
Shannon Osborn
Helen Pagel
Lisa Ann Parkes
Russ Parkes
Celia and Earl Parrott
Kile Patrick
Betsy Peebles
Beverly Pigg
Gerrie and John Porter
Stasia Porter
LaRue V. Pryor
Julia Pulliam
Anna Quinn
Harriette Quin
Frances Rainey
Kip Reel
Lisa Riddle
Celia Ridley
Patty Ridley
Suzie Sanders
Argie Satterwhite
Martha Schulz
Peggy Sciotto
Tina Seago
Jim Sewell
Ingrid Shapiro
Virginia Sharpe
Bettye Sharpton
Carolyn Sims
Gerri Sisco
Susan G. Sloan
Pamela Smith
Dorothy Sowell
Frances Sowell

Lillie Sowell
Polly Stanton
Betty Steenbergen
Jane Stephens
Leesa Stevens
Peggy Sullivan
Carolyn Suschnick
Edie Sutter
Norma P. Thomas
Nancy Thompson
Ora Thompson
Sarah Thompson
Cindy Toler
Delia Tietgens
Wanda K. Turner
Karen Vest
Melba Vest
Dinah Vire
Suzie Wagster
Linda Walter
Lolly Watson
Mary Webb
Marilyn Webster
Ann West
Julia West
Barbara Wiesman
Margaret Wiley
Pauline Wilkes
Jerry Williams
Kay Kay Williams
Nanette Williams
Mary Neil Wise
Reda Witherow
Nell Woodard
Ann York
Lesa Young

ACKNOWLEDGMENTS

*John Holtzapple and Thomas Price of the Polk Home staff wrote the
vignettes on Sarah Polk using information from the Home's collection of original
documents as well as these other sources:*

Correspondence of James K. Polk (ed. by Herbert Weaver and Wayne Cutler)
The Diary of James K. Polk During His Presidency (ed. by Milo M. Quaife)
First Ladies by Betty Boyd Caroli
The First Ladies Cook Book by Margaret Brown Klapthor and Helen Duprey Bullock
James K. Polk, Jacksonian and James K. Polk, Continentalist by Charles Sellers
Less Time for Meddling: A History of Salem Academy and College by Frances Green
Memorials of Sarah Childress Polk by Anson and Fanny Nelson
The Papers of Andrew Johnson (ed. by Paul H. Bergeron)
The President's House by William Seale
Sarah Childress Polk: A Biography of the Remarkable First Lady by John Reed Bumgarner
The Southern Plantation Overseer by John Spencer Bassett

BENEFACTORS

Community First Bank and Trust
Mr. and Mrs. Don Crichton
First Farmers and Merchants National Bank
The James K. Polk Memorial Association of Nashville
Mr. and Mrs. H. W. Lucas
Middle Tennessee Visitors Bureau
Mr. and Mrs. John Cheairs Porter
Southern Radiology Associates

INDEX

191